TEACHING THE AMERICAN PEOPLE
A Guide for Instructors
to accompany

NASH·JEFFREY
HOWE · FREDERICK · DAVIS · WINKLER

THE AMERICAN PEOPLE

CREATING A NATION AND A SOCIETY

Second Edition

JULIE ROY JEFFREY
Goucher College

PETER J. FREDERICK
Wabash College

HARPER & ROW, PUBLISHERS, New York
Grand Rapids, Philadelphia, St. Louis, San Francisco,
London, Singapore, Sydney, Tokyo

TEACHING THE AMERICAN PEOPLE: A Guide for Instructor's to accompany THE AMERICAN PEOPLE: Creating a Nation and a Society, 2/e

Copyright © 1990 by Harper & Row, Publishers, Inc.

ISBN: 0-06-364754-0

90 91 92 93   9 8 7 6 5 4 3 2 1

"I believe that the greatest challenge confronting historians today is the challenge of the classroom. To meet it we shall have to give to teaching a higher place in our scale of values than we do today.... And--it goes without saying--we shall ourselves have to be the best teachers that we know how to be, the most humane, the most sympathetic, the most dedicated."

> --Dexter Perkins, A.H.A. Presidential Address
> December 19, 1956

Acknowledgements

Our ideas about teaching and learning have several sources, but none so important as those interactions and friendships with our students over the past 25 years at Rice University, California State University at Hayward, Goucher College, the University of Vienna, and Wabash College. In particular, we are grateful for the invaluable help of three student assistants, Jane Golberg, George T. Patton, and Zhen-ming Tan, whose knowledge, insights, and computer skills were invaluable in preparing the study guides and this volume for teachers. They have already begun to teach a new generation of history students.

"I am suggesting that unless we restore to the teaching of history at every level that humanistic aspect that sees history primarily as the story of people living in a distant time and in another place--unless we do that we lose the greatest strength that history has to offer....Teaching history well is one of the best things a person can do."

> --Gerda Lerner, O. A. H. Address to
> Teachers, April, 1986

CONTENTS

INTRODUCTION

Since it is unusual for the authors of a history textbook also to prepare its supporting pedagogical materials, we would like to explain why we decided to write this volume and the study guides. Like all historians, we believe that it is important for college students to learn about their past and are dismayed by the pattern of declining history enrollments. By writing a text that attempts to make the past vivid for students by putting them inside the lives of ordinary people, that highlights important themes in American history, and that stresses their human meaning, we hope to contribute to a reversal of current trends. We believe that students enjoy and appreciate history more when they have lively classroom experiences, an understanding of the significance of history for their own lives, and a sense of confidence in their abilities to learn about the past.

But we also realize that many students need help in approaching and understanding a textbook. Therefore, since as authors we know this text well, we have prepared the study guides ourselves. A lively classroom, a sense of confidence, and an understanding and appreciation of history all depend on students spending enough time reading and thinking about the text. We have written the guides to supplement the text in order to help students read the textbook intelligently. Each chapter of the study guides highlights the main themes and features of that chapter and includes important factual and conceptual knowledge we think students should know. In addition, we have suggested further activities that we think will enrich their efforts to understand the past. We encourage students to work back and forth from the chapter in The American People to the chapter in the guide, thereby reinforcing and strengthening their mastery of the material.

1

The first three sections of each chapter in the study guides also appear in this volume, but the rest is rather different. It would be helpful if instructors looked quickly through the study guides to familiarize themselves with the parts not included here, in particular the introductory material ("How to Pass Your History Course by Rediscovering the Past") and the sample test and examination questions at the end of each chapter. (The students also have sections titled "Important Dates and Names to Know" and "Glossary of Important Terms," the contents of which are obvious.) Please note especially that we have arranged the test questions from lower-order multiple-choice and matching memory questions on factual knowledge to those involving higher-order, analytical skills. A glance at the variety of examples of these various sorts of questions might facilitate your own writing of tests and examinations. (The publisher has also made available a Test Bank in both printed and computer formats.)

Since we are both involved in full-time undergraduate teaching, we are aware of the many pressures--and rewards--of college teaching. We have, therefore, tried to write a teachable textbook, including the support guides, to enhance your efforts and those of your students. This volume is intended to help you make the hours of preparing for classes and teaching The American People as significant, enriching, and enjoyable as possible. In no way do we mean to prescribe classroom methods or to suggest that any one model of teaching is better than others. We all have our own distinctive styles. But we do want to suggest ways of increasing your teaching options as you plan your American history classes.

We have called this volume Teaching the American People not just because of the double meaning of the phrase but also because we think the textbook can become an integral part of your course. In Teaching the American People we have sought to suggest specific ways in which the text might be used to enliven your classroom and improve your students' learning and appreciation of American history.

We have looked at many instructors' manuals. The teaching suggestions in them are usually confined to ideas for lectures. We have discovered in our own teaching careers that it is often easier to lecture than to risk interactive, participatory classroom activities. But we have also experienced the joys of using innovative active learning strategies to enliven and enrich history for both students and ourselves. Therefore, without excluding lecture topics, Teaching the American People describes diverse ways of generating class discussions and involving college students in active, participatory learning. Many of these enrichment strategies will work with large as well as small classes; we have therefore suggested ways of breaking large groups into

2

smaller ones or have otherwise indicated how the lecture hall format can be adapted to permit student participation.

The Structure of <u>Teaching the American People</u>

Each chapter in this book contains the following five sections:

CHAPTER OUTLINE (with opening anecdote)

The chapter outline enables you and your students to see at a glance the major topics and organization of the chapter. The short summary of the personal anecdote that begins each chapter is highlighted because these stories suggest the main themes and special features of the chapter. Chapter 1, for example, begins with the tragic account of Opechancanough, a Native American whose entire life of over 90 years was consumed by a losing struggle against the land hunger and alien values brought by Spanish and English newcomers to his ancestral lands near the Chesapeake Bay. The brief anecdote about Opechancanough serves to introduce the crucial concept of the convergence of three worlds--red, white, and black--each with different life styles, cultural values, and aspirations. Opechancanough's capture and death at the hands of an English jailer in 1646 foreshadowed the destruction of Native Americans and their way of life by Europeans in coming centuries. The paragraphs immediately following the anecdote in each chapter are especially crucial in showing the major themes and organizational structure of the chapter. Students need help in learning how to read those key paragraphs, perhaps by showing them how during class early in the term.

SIGNIFICANT THEMES AND HIGHLIGHTS

In this section, three or four statements, introduced by the anecdote, provide an overview of the main themes, concepts, threads, major ideas, and special features of each chapter. These statements highlight the lives of persons whose experiences are woven throughout several chapters, thus underlining the human dimensions of the text. They also clarify the chapter author's interpretation of the events covered in the chapter. These, too, are crucial and should be highlighted for students.

LEARNING GOALS OF THE CHAPTER

A list of goals, or objectives, for each chapter provides you (and your students) with a quick sense of the substance of the chapter and outlines material that students should learn. This section sets forth two kinds of goals. The first deals with the basic facts every history student should know and is labeled, "Familiarity with Basic Knowledge." These necessary but lower-order learning tasks can be tested with short-answer quiz and exam questions. The second set of goals, entitled "Practice in Historical Thinking Skills," outlines higher-order learning tasks such as analyzing, comparing and contrasting, applying, and evaluating historical phenomena. These skills can be tested by essay questions, paper assignments, and class discussions. This is a key section for students to review when they prepare for a test, and you may want to refer to it when you construct exams.

ENRICHMENT IDEAS

We think this is the most important section in these guides. For many students, personal involvement may be the most forceful basis for observation and reflection about the past. This section, therefore, contains a list of activities and experiences, some described in more detail than others, intended to deepen students' understanding of the major themes of the chapter by inviting them to participate actively in their own learning. The first few suggestions students can follow and do on their own, although they would be improved by your adaptations. Beyond these suggestions are several, found in this volume only, that are provided for teachers.

The learning enrichment section includes: ideas for discussion, debate, and lecture; suggestions for films, slides, music, and other methods using sight and sound; written assignments or role-playing exercises in which students are invited to imagine themselves into the lives of the people they are studying; field trips and museum visits; small group activities, also adapted to large classes; family and community history projects; and other ways of enriching historical learning. The ideas found in this section are both traditional and innovative; all can of course be adapted by instructors to their own style and situation. We particularly recommend the Harper & Row companion set of two volumes, <u>Retracing the Past: Readings in the History of the</u>

<u>American People</u>, edited by Gary B. Nash, to enrich the textbook for both instructors and students.

The first enrichment suggestion for each chapter focuses on the "Recovering the Past" feature in the textbook, a section that introduces students to the many sources and ways historians find out what happened in the past. This section also helps students learn how to ask questions and provides active experiences to help them develop the confidence that they can be their own historians in "recovering the past." The following list identifies the "RTPs" for each chapter:

Chapter	**Topic**
1. Three Worlds Meet	Archaeological Artifacts
2. Colonizing a Continent	Houses
3. Mastering the New World	Tombstones
4. The Maturing of Colonial Society	Tax Records
5. Bursting the Colonial Bonds	Household Inventories
6. A People in Revolution	Military Muster Rolls
7. Consolidating the Revolution	Indian Treaties
8. Creating a Nation	Patriotic Paintings
9. Politics and Society in the Early Republic	Maps
10. The Preindustrial Republic	Census Returns
11. Currents of Change in the Northeast and Old Northwest	Family Paintings
12. Slavery and the Old South	Folktales
13. Shaping America in the Antebellum Age	European Travel Journals
14. Moving West	Private Sources: Diaries
15. The Union in Peril	Senate Speeches
16. The Union Severed	Photography
17. The Union Reconstructed	Novels
18. The Farmer's World	Magazines
19. The Rise of Smokestack America	Congressional Hearings
20. Politics and Reform	Material Culture: Political Campaign Artifacts
21. Becoming a World Power	Political Cartoons
22. The Progressives Confront Industrial Capitalism	Documentary Photographs
23. The Great War	Government Propaganda
24. Affluence and Anxiety	Advertising
25. The Great Depression and the New Deal	The Movies
26. World War II	Oral History
27. Chills and Fever During the Cold War	Public Opinion Polls
28. Postwar Growth and Social Change	Popular Music

29. Politics and Governmental Power   Cartoon Humor
30. The Struggle for Social Reform   Television
31. The United States Since 1976:
    Redefining the American Dream   Autobiography

For the most part, each means of recovering the past is appropriate to the content of the chapter in which it appears. Thus the use of archaeology in understanding earlier civilizations is discussed in Chapter 1; folktales in the chapter on slavery; and films, oral history, and television in the appropriate twentieth-century chapters. This list of RTPs, it should be added, is only suggestive, not complete. Although students are encouraged to think about and work with the RTPs on their own, these sections lend themselves to classroom use, as adapted by you according to your particular context. Working with an RTP in class is a good way of getting students to bring their texts to class and provides the common focused inquiry that aids learning.

FURTHER RESOURCES

In this section, not included in the student guides, we list supplemental audiovisual resources appropriate to the chapter. We include educational and documentary films, slide and photograph collections, and records or audio cassettes of music and speeches. We have also included a selected address list of distributors of films and other media at the end. A set of selected color map and chart transparencies is available from the publisher, as are other pedagogical aids.

TEACHING HISTORY

The volume concludes with two items that we think add to the value of The American People. The first is a short bibliography of references about teaching. The second is a reprint of an article by Peter Frederick called "The Lively Lecture: Eight Variations," published in 1986 in College Teaching. The article complements Frederick's "The Dreaded Discussion: Ten Ways to Start," which was included in the first edition of Teaching the American People. At the many workshops on teaching and learning for college instructors we have led over the past decade, we have found that getting students motivated and involved is the most difficult thing teachers do. Faculty have found both articles challenging and full of practical, usable ideas. We have added a summary list of active learning strategies for history used in our workshops.

Perhaps the most useful suggestions for teaching are found in the Enrichment sections for each chapter, where we have adapted many of Peter Frederick's ideas for large classes. By focusing on teaching strategies for each chapter, you can help students learn the particular content of that chapter. As a result, your students' informed appreciation and enjoyment of history is enhanced. It is this goal, we firmly believe, that is the primary purpose of <u>Teaching the American People.</u> Have a good semester!

PJF & JRJ

PART ONE

A COLONIZING PEOPLE
1492–1776

1

Three Worlds Meet

(1) CHAPTER OUTLINE

For his entire life of 90 years in the Chesapeake Bay region, the Powhatan tribesman Opechancanough struggled to defend his land and way of life against the intrusions of the Spanish and English (and even Africans), thus showing how the lives of red, white, and black people were intertwined in North America.

The People of America Before Columbus

>Hunters and Farmers
>Native Americans in 1600
>Contrasting World Views

Africa on the Eve of Contact

>The Kingdoms of Africa
>The African Ethos

Europe in the Age of Exploration

>The Rise of Europe
>The New Monarchies and the Expansionist Impulse
>Reaching the Americas
>Religious Conflict During the Reformation

The Iberian Conquest of America

    The Spanish Onslaught
    The Great Dying
    Silver, Sugar, and Their Consequences
    Spain's Northern Frontier

England Goes West

    England Challenges Spain
    The Westward Fever
    Anticipating North America

Conclusion: Converging Worlds

(2) SIGNIFICANT THEMES AND HIGHLIGHTS

1. The clash of three cultures from three continents --North America, Europe, and Africa--forms the opening chapter of American history and is therefore the opening chapter of the textbook. In Opechancanough's life story we see the collision and intermingling of three worlds, red, white, and black. The converging of cultural values and aspirations, often accompanied by violence and disease, disrupted and nearly destroyed the red world, enslaved the victims from the black world, and furthered the expansion and development of the white world.

2. A secondary clash within the European white world, that between Catholic Spain and Protestant England, explains the different development of Spanish Central and South America and English North America.

3. By taking readers inside the cultural beliefs and experiences of Native Americans and Africans, as well as Europeans, this chapter serves to counteract the traditional ethnocentric view that sees all developments through the eyes of Europeans. An example of this is the oft-repeated phrase, "Columbus discovered America," implying that there was no life or culture in the Americas until a European found it in 1492.

(3) LEARNING GOALS

Familiarity with Basic Knowledge

After reading this chapter, you should be able to:

1. Locate and briefly describe the Native American Mound Builders of the Ohio and Mississippi river valleys, the Pueblo dwellers of the Southwest, and the woodland Indians of the East Coast.

2. Describe Native American attitudes toward and beliefs about the natural world, wealth, community, family, and men and women.

3. Name and locate three West African kingdoms between the fifth and fourteenth centuries and describe West African beliefs about family, religion, and social organization.

4. Explain the political, economic, religious, and technological changes in early modern Europe that led to the exploration and eventual settlement of North America.

5. Locate on a map the names and routes of the most significant Iberian, English, French, and Dutch explorers and conquerors in the fifteenth and sixteenth centuries.

6. Describe the impact of the European conquest of the Americas on the Native American Indian population.

Practice in Historical Thinking Skills

After reading this chapter, you should be able to:

1. Compare and contrast the values and life styles of the three worlds--red, white, and black--that met in the Americas early in the sixteenth century.

2. Evaluate the outcomes of that collision for each world. What do you think and feel about these outcomes?

3. Compare and contrast the cultures of Spain and England, and their motivations for settling the Americas.

(4) ENRICHMENT IDEAS

1. Find out which Native American tribes and nations
    lived in your part of the country and whether there
    are any archaeological working sites or remains, like
    Cahokia, to visit. Also visit any museums or
    historical parks that feature local Indian history.

2. Pretend that you are an archaeologist or
    anthropologist who wants to understand and
    reconstruct in your region as much of the original
    Indian culture and typical daily life as possible
    from relics and other remains. Present your findings
    to others in various forms: oral report, written
    paper, table display showing artifacts and a model of
    Indian life, or artistic drawings or skits
    illustrating Indian culture.

3. Pretend that you are an archaeologist or
    anthropologist from some distant future who wants to
    understand and reconstruct as much as possible of
    present-day culture and daily life in your community.
    Imagine the absolute destruction of all written
    records and the near-destruction and burying under
    dirt and debris of material objects and structures.
    As you dig up the remains or observe unusual
    topological and other features (like dammed-up
    streams, terraced and flattened hills, or roadway
    patterns), how much of the original daily life and
    culture do you think you could reconstruct?

4. Imagine yourself as a Martian, who has never seen
    Earthlings, arriving to explore and settle the planet
    Earth. From the behavior of human beings what kind of
    conclusions might you draw about their cultural
    patterns and values? What images do you have about
    groups different from your own? Think about both
    positive and negative images.

5. Look over the opening anecdote. Imagine yourself as
    Opechancanough going through the various epochs of
    his life. Write a speech or memoir on what he might
    have thought about the values and cultural norms of
    white people in the various seasons of his life.

Instructor:

6. Ideas 1-5 are suitable for out-of-class assignments
    or in-class lectures, discussions, and presentations.
    The goals here are primarily to involve students in

research (or some reflection) on the Native Americans who lived in their part of the country, to introduce them to the historical usefulness of the work of archaeologists and anthropologists, and to help students experience and perhaps understand the limitations and dangers of an ethnocentric view of other cultures.

7. Students may be influenced more by how this first chapter is treated than by any other, so teachers have a great opportunity to begin well. They can use this chapter to help students learn how to underline, read, and study a textbook chapter. It shows how the anecdote suggests major themes and structures of a chapter. But in addition, this particular chapter raises three important questions for students to think about during the rest of the course: (1) the clash of red, white, and black cultures in the Americas; (2) ethnocentrism and how various historical interpretations change over time, in this case perspectives on the interaction between Europeans and Native Americans; and (3) how a creative use of new sources and other disciplines can aid us in recovering the past.

8. Beginning the course with a film or filmstrip (see section 5) on Native American cultures prior to the arrival of Europeans will highlight the point that America was not "discovered" first by voyagers from Europe.

9. An excellent lecture topic is to show the demographic impact of European conquest of the Americas on the Native American population and to contrast the treatment of this population by Spanish and English explorers and settlers. Chapters 1 and 4 in Volume One of <u>Retracing the Past: Readings in the History of the American People</u>, edited by Gary B. Nash, are excellent sources.

(5) FURTHER RESOURCES

Documentaries and Films

1. <u>In Search of the Lost World</u> (52 mins.; Native American cultural development)

2. <u>The Early Americans</u> (41 mins.; migration of first Americans)

3. Archaeology: Furnace Brook Site (19 mins.; explores prehistoric Iroquois village)

4. The First Americans (53 mins.; archaeological exploration of Native Americans)

5. Reformation (52 mins.; sweep of Lutheran and Calvinist ideas across Europe)

6. Towards a Modern Europe (30 mins.; conditions that prepared Europe for modernity)

7. Alistair Cooke's America: A Personal History of the United States, Episode 1, The New Found Land (55 mins.)

8. England of Elizabeth (26 mins.; Elizabethan culture)

9. Stop Ruining America's Past (21 mins.; film emphasizing the importance of archaeology, using Cahokia Mounds and Hopewell Mounds as the focus)

Slides and Filmstrips

1. American History Slide Collection (Instructional Resources Corporation, Laurel, Maryland), groups A ("Explorers and Early America") and C ("American Indians")

2. An Introduction to the Indians of America (Morey Associates, Kansas City, Missouri), in five parts, each one showing both the distinctive different regional Native American cultures and the effects on those cultures of the arrival of white Europeans: 1. Indians of the Great Plains (24 mins.); 2. Indians of the Southwest (21 mins.); 3. Indians of the Northwest (20 mins.); 4. Indians of the Northeast (18 mins.); 5. Indians of the Southeast (18 mins.)

3. Discovery and Exploration, five filmstrips from the American Heritage Media Collection

2

Colonizing a Continent

(1) CHAPTER OUTLINE

Captain John Mason leaves the Massachusetts Bay Colony with other Puritans in search of better lands. They establish the new community of Windsor on the Connecticut River. Shortly afterward, Mason leads hundreds of the settlers in an attack on the Pequot Indians, massacring them.

The Chesapeake Tobacco Coast

> Jamestown
> Sot Weed and Indentured Servants
> Expansion and Indian War
> Proprietary Maryland
> Daily Life on the Chesapeake

Massachusetts and Its Offspring

> Puritanism in England
> Puritan Predecessors in New England
> Errand into the Wilderness
> An Elusive Utopia
> New Englanders and Indians
> The Web of Village Life

From the St. Lawrence to the Hudson

> England Challenges the Mighty Dutch

14

Proprietary Carolina: A Restoration Reward
The Indian Debacle
Early Carolina Society

The Quakers' Peaceable Kingdom

The Early Friends
Early Quaker Designs
Pacifism in a Militant World:
Quakers and Indians
Building the Peaceable Kingdom
The Limits of Perfectionism

Conclusion: The Achievement of New Societies

(2) SIGNIFICANT THEMES AND HIGHLIGHTS

1. A theme running throughout the chapter, illustrated
    by the Pequot massacre, is the confrontation in North
    America between two cultures: the English colonists
    (in various kinds of settlements) and the Native
    American Indians. The two cultures collided as the
    colonists sought to realize the goals that had lured
    them to the New World and the Native Americans sought
    to defend their tribal homelands.

2. A second theme focuses on tensions growing out of the
    religious and economic motivations behind settlement.
    Many English colonists came to America to create
    religious utopias, a New World Zion. Others, even in
    the same settlement, came for economic opportunity,
    gold, and land. Regardless of motive, the colonists
    experienced limits to their aspirations: Both utopia
    and economic opportunity proved elusive, the former
    far more than the latter.

3. Another recurrent theme of the chapter is the tension
    between religious idealism and violence. The
    colonial world was a violent one, both in contact
    with the Native Americans and in the social conflicts
    that emerged in the difficult early years of
    settlement.

4. The English colonists not only clashed with Native
    American cultures but also developed various
    cultures themselves. This chapter is structured
    around the reconstruction of the modes of settlement
    and character of life in five distinctly different
    societies along the Atlantic Coast: the Chesapeake

region of Virginia and Maryland, Puritan New England, New York under the Dutch and English, Proprietary Carolina, and Quaker Pennsylvania. In the account of each society is a picture of daily life as reflected in the architecture of houses, material household belongings, patterns of family life, and the role of women.

(3) LEARNING GOALS

Familiarity with Basic Knowledge

After reading this chapter, you should be able to:

1. Locate the various distinct settlements on a map of the Atlantic Coast, in particular Jamestown and the Chesapeake Bay tobacco area, Roanoke Island, Charleston, Plymouth, Boston and Massachusetts Bay, New York, the Hudson River, Delaware, the Connecticut and James rivers, and Philadelphia and the greater Pennsylvania settlement.

2. Describe the changing population, social patterns, and daily life of the Chesapeake tobacco coast in the seventeenth century.

3. Describe the beliefs, social patterns, and the character of village life of the New England Puritans in England in early seventeenth-century Massachusetts.

4. Outline the major features of economic and social life in seventeenth-century New York and Carolina.

5. Describe Quaker beliefs and the efforts to build a peaceable kingdom in William Penn's settlement in Pennsylvania.

Practice in Historical Thinking Skills

After reading this chapter, you should be able to:

1. Compare and contrast the reasons and motivations for the settlement of each of the five main colonies, and describe the relationship of each of the five settlements with the Native Americans of that region.

2. Reconstruct and compare the essentials of daily life, including the lives of women, in each of the five

settlements in the seventeenth century.

3. Discuss whether you think utopian idealism or economic necessity was a more important motivation in the settlement and development of the English colonies.

(4) ENRICHMENT IDEAS

1. As an extension of the RTP in this chapter, recall the differences in housing between Massachusetts Bay and the Chesapeake region. How do the houses and their furnishings show the differences and similarities in the two societies? Find examples of house design in Maryland and Virginia in the early eighteenth century. What are the significant differences between the earlier Chesapeake housing and these? What do the newer designs reveal about social and economic changes? You can also compare the Boardmen house to eighteenth-century Massachusetts houses to see what kind of changes have taken place there.

2. As a class project, make replicas or plans of typical villages from each settlement. This can include everything from designs on paper to miniature villages on tabletops fashioned out of Popsicle sticks and the like. Note how house designs reflect daily life in the various settlements.

3. Write a letter or diary entry describing the daily life of a typical inhabitant on a typical day in three or four of the five settlements in seventeenth century America.

4. Construct an imaginary document reflecting each settlement's attitude toward and relationship with the area's Native American tribes. The document might be a sermon, a treaty, a leader's policy statement, a letter by a young man or woman in the settlement, or a speech (or letter) by a young Indian of the appropriate area.

5. Imagine yourself to be an indentured servant in the Chesapeake. Were you to write a letter home to a brother or sister, how would you describe your life? Would you encourage your brother or sister to come to the New World?

<u>Instructor:</u>

6. John Demos's <u>Little Commonwealth</u> provides a
   provocative picture of daily life in
   seventeenth-century Plymouth. This monograph lends
   itself to a lecture on or discussion of family
   structures, gender roles, and the use of artifacts,
   court cases, and wills as historical sources for
   details of everyday life.

7. Give students shipboard lists (found in Donald M.
   Scott and Bernard Wishy, eds., <u>America's Families: A
   Documentary History</u>) of passengers headed for
   Massachusetts Bay and the Chesapeake. By studying
   these lists, students can see the various
   demographic characteristics of the different groups
   of settlers and speculate on social results. This
   idea can be adapted for large classes by the use of
   an overhead projector, with the instructor providing
   the analysis.

8. Parts of the trial of Anne Hutchinson can be acted
   out for the purpose of discussion. (Excerpts can be
   found in Nancy Cott's <u>Roots of Bitterness</u>, and the
   entire record in David Hall, <u>The Antinomian
   Controversy</u>). Students can see and discuss various
   levels of the conflict--religious, political, and
   sexual. This exercise lends itself to a
   presentation to a large group, followed by breaking
   into smaller groups for discussion.

(5) FURTHER RESOURCES

Documentaries and Films

1. <u>Alistair Cooke's America</u>. Episode 2, <u>Home Away from
   Home</u> (55 mins.)

2. <u>The American Idea</u> (21 mins.; examination of early
   colonial New England ideals and life through
   interviews with descendants in a Vermont town)

3. <u>Anne Hutchinson: Profiles in Courage</u> (50 mins.)

4. <u>Fare You Well, Old Houses: Dutch Houses of the
   Hackensack River Valley</u> (30 mins.)

Filmstrips

England Stakes a Claim; Religious Havens, The American Melting Pot, from the American Heritage Media Collection

3

Mastering the New World

(1) CHAPTER OUTLINE

Anthony and Mary Johnson, two freed slaves, live in the uneasy world between freedom and slavery. Although the family initially prospers, as attitudes toward blacks harden they find fewer and fewer opportunities available to them. The Johnson children and grandchildren are unable to match the modest success of Anthony and Mary.

Black Bondage

The Slave Trade
The Southern Transition to Black Labor
Slavery in the Northern Colonies
The System of Bondage

Slave Culture

The Growth of Slavery
Resistance and Rebellion
Black Religion and Family

The Struggle for Land

King Philip's War in New England
Bacon's Rebellion Engulfs Virginia

An Era of Instability

>Organizing the Empire
>The Glorious Revolution in New England
>Leisler's Rebellion in New York
>Southern Rumblings
>The Social Basis of Politics
>Witchcraft in Salem

Contending for a Continent

>Anglo-French Rivalry
>The Results of War

Conclusion: Controlling the New Environment

(2) SIGNIFICANT THEMES AND HIGHLIGHTS

1. This chapter treats five conflicts in the colonial period between 1675 and 1715: two dealt with the European colonial effort to establish mastery over African slaves and Native American Indians; two concerned administrative and class struggles among the English colonists themselves; the final one was an international struggle as the British sought mastery over French, Dutch, and Spanish colonial contenders.

2. Although the boundaries of American slavery were at first fluid, as the Johnsons' experience showed, the institution of slavery altered the shape of American society. Slavery became a primary source of labor and profits in the Chesapeake but was also closely bound up with economic life in the North. Slavery profoundly affected the lives of both white and black Americans and was an ironic comment on the dream of America as a place of refuge and hope. The personal stories of Olaudah Equiano and the Johnson clan convey some of the pain connected with slavery and the status of blacks.

3. At the same time that racial boundaries between blacks and whites were hardening, the violent battle of whites for Native American lands continued. The struggle is described in New England, the Chesapeake, and South Carolina. Although losses were heavy for both Native Americans and white settlers, in the end, the coastal tribes were defeated.

21

4. Small insurrections against colonial administrators and elites, triggered by the Glorious Revolution of 1688, erupted in several colonies. Although they were in no way a "dress rehearsal" for the American Revolution, they did reveal some of the social and political tensions growing out of the attempt to plant English society in the New World.

5. Soon after these insurrections, Europe plunged into war. Rivalries of the Old World affected the New even though the major battlefields were, in fact, far away from the colonies. The impact of European events on the colonies is another indication of the close bonds between the new society and the old.

(3) LEARNING GOALS

Familiarity with Basic Knowledge

After reading this chapter, you should be able to:

1. Describe the slave trade and explain three ways in which the presence of black slaves altered the direction of American society.

2. Give three reasons for the transformation of the Chesapeake labor force in the late seventeenth century.

3. Describe some features of the culture of African-Americans in the seventeenth century.

4. Describe the course and consequences of King Philip's War in New England and Bacon's Rebellion in Virginia.

5. Outline the steps leading to the Glorious Revolution and briefly explain what it was.

6. State three basic differences between the French and English settlements in North America.

Practice in Historical Thinking Skills

After reading this chapter, you should be able to:

1. Analyze how the conflicts among Englishmen and Africans and Native Americans, among Englishmen themselves, and between the British and other

European nations changed the relations among white, black, and red people in the New World.

2. Show the most important effects of the Glorious Revolution in England and of European national rivalries on the colonies in the late seventeenth and early eighteenth centuries.

3. Explain why the late seventeenth century has been described as a period of great instability and change in American history.

(4) ENRICHMENT IDEAS

1. After working with the questions in the RTP about how tombstones reveal changing attitudes, especially toward religion, design some tombstones of your own, including both epitaph (inscription) and iconography (pictorial design). Make one or two for the mid-seventeenth century and one or two for the early eighteenth century. Finally, design a modern tombstone, perhaps for yourself or a friend, showing how epitaphs and iconography reflect contemporary attitudes and values.

2. Chart the main events in Anthony Johnson's life and the lives of his children. Then try to imagine how Anthony would explain each of the most important events. How might he explain the changing nature of race relations? What advice would you give to Johnson and his family?

3. In what ways does this chapter suggest that racism is a continuing part of American life? Which came first in American society, racism or slavery? What relevance does this chapter have for today? What social or international conflicts still go on between peoples?

Instructor:

4. The "Slave" episode from Roots focuses on the middle passage and can provide the basis for class discussions on the clash of Christian morality with one's livelihood as a slave trader, the survival of African culture among slaves in the Americas, and the historical validity of the TV docudrama.

23

5. A lecture on the formation of racist attitudes can be drawn from Winthrop D. Jordan's <u>White Over Black: American Racial Attitudes Toward the Negro, 1550-1812.</u>

6. The historic house offers many possibilities for assignments and in-class exercises. House plans offer other possibilities. There are many ways to use house plans. You might have students study the arrangement of space and speculate on what spatial arrangements suggest about work, leisure, gender roles, and opportunities for privacy. The floor plans of a New England farmhouse reveal the nature of the family economy and highlight women's role as producers. For a large class, the instructor can provide an interesting slide lecture.

7. Have students describe and analyze the events of Bacon's Rebellion from the perspective of Governor Berkeley and his council, Bacon's followers, and braves from the Susquehannock tribe. Have each version of events presented, and ask other students to choose the most compelling position and explain their reasons for their choice. This can be done in any size class (even large lectures) by dividing the class into thirds, asking them to think their way into their respective roles, inviting several statements from each third of the class, and perhaps concluding with a vote on which side's case was most persuasively presented.

8. Although the chapter focuses on the emergence of slave culture, there were several factors retarding its development (the isolated situation of many early slaves, the slow formation of slave families, etc.). A lecture on the early conditions of slavery in the Chesapeake and in the North could provide the backdrop for the consideration of slave culture (see James Deetz, <u>In Small Things Forgotten</u>, the works of Allan Kulikoff for the Chesapeake, and Chapter 5 in Gary Nash's <u>Retracing the Past</u>, Volume One).

9. Students might enjoy reading Arthur Miller's <u>The Crucible</u> (even acting out scenes) and comparing Miller's interpretation of witchcraft in Salem to that presented here. John Demos's <u>Entertaining Satan</u> suggests a unique approach to the study of witchcraft that can provide the basis for lectures and class discussions.

(5) FURTHER RESOURCES

Documentaries and Films

1. <u>The Witches of Salem: The Horror and the Hope</u> (35 mins.; a dramatization of an authentic 1692 trial)

2. <u>Roots,</u> episodes 1 and 2

3. <u>From the Bottom Up</u> (28 mins.; Minnesota Historical Society's underwater archaeology program recovers fur trade artifacts)

Slides and Filmstrips

1. <u>American History Slide Collection</u>, groups C ("American Indians") and H ("Black America"; slave trade)

2. <u>African Art and Culture</u>, three filmstrips: "Early Art," "Sculpture," and "Masks" (Warren Schloat Productions)

4

The Maturing of Colonial Society

(1) CHAPTER OUTLINE

During a period of rapid growth, Devereaux Jarratt grows up in the family of a Virginia yeoman farmer. His interest in books and learning enables him to become a tutor for rich Virginia planter families. Eventually he rises to become an Anglican clergyman.

America's First Population Explosion

> The New Immigrants
> New Classes of Newcomers
> A Land of Opportunity?
> Africans in Chains

Beyond the Appalachians

> Cultural Changes Among Interior Tribes
> France's Inland Empire
> Spain's America

A Land of Family Farms

> Northern Agricultural Society
> Changing Values
> Women in Northern Colonial Society

The Plantation South

The Tobacco Coast
The Rice Coast
The Backcountry
Family Life in the South

The Urban World of Commerce and Ideas

Sinews of Trade
The Artisans' World
Urban Social Structure
The Entrepreneurial Ethos
The American Enlightenment

The Great Awakening

Fading Faith
The Awakeners' Message
The Urban North
The Rural South
Legacy of the Awakening

Political Life

Structuring Colonial Governments
The Crowd in Action
The Growing Power of the Assemblies
Local Politics
The Spread of Whig Ideology

Conclusion: America in 1750

(2) SIGNIFICANT THEMES AND HIGHLIGHTS

1. In the first half of the eighteenth century, America
   was made up of several distinct regional societies,
   each in the process of growth and change. Beyond the
   Appalachians, extensive contact with France's growing
   inland empire and Spanish American settlements in the
   South and Southwest transformed Native American
   life. English settlements, however, exploding in
   population, threatened Indian cultural cohesion the
   most. This chapter stresses the increasing
   complexity, adaption, and maturing of colonial
   English society. The eighteenth century provided
   opportunities for some, like Devereaux Jarratt; great
   gains for a few, like Boston merchant Andrew Belcher;
   but disappointment and privation for many others.

2. The farming society of the North was characterized by
    widespread land ownership and a rough kind of
    economic equality. In the South, plantation society
    was marked by the emergence of a gentry class and a
    labor force almost entirely made up of black slaves,
    while the backcountry, still in the frontier stages
    and settled by thousands of Scots-Irish and German
    immigrants, lacked the sharp class distinctions of
    the tidewater region. Colonial cities, with their
    highly differentiated class structure and new
    commercial values, were on the "cutting edge" of
    change. In each area, women played an important but
    limited role in daily life.

3. The Great Awakening was more than a religious
    revival, for it produced patterns of thought and
    behavior that helped to fuel the Revolution. The
    course of the Great Awakening in Boston and Virginia
    vividly shows the way in which its message fused with
    local social and economic tensions to threaten
    established authority.

4. Although many historians focus on the changing
    political arrangements in the colonies in the first
    half of the eighteenth century as a means of
    preparing for a discussion of the Revolution, this
    chapter makes the point that the fluidity of American
    society itself must be understood as a prelude to the
    events of the 1770s.

(3) LEARNING GOALS

Familiarity with Basic Knowledge

After reading this chapter, you should be able to:

1. Name the major immigrant groups coming to the
    colonies in the early eighteenth century, describe
    their social background, find their destinations on
    the map, and summarize their relative opportunities
    for social and economic advancement.

2. Describe the cultural changes of the interior Native
    American tribes as a result of their contact with
    French, Spanish, and English settlements in economic,
    social, and domestic life; in their relation to the
    environment; in political organization; and in
    intertribal tensions.

3. Describe northern farm society and its most important social characteristics and problems, including family life and the ways in which the roles and rights of women changed in the colonies.

4. Give an account of the "profound social transition" of the Upper South, characterize the social and political nature of the southern gentry, and detail the social and economic differences between the tobacco and rice coasts and the backcountry.

5. Describe the urban social structure, including the merchant's pivotal role, and the work pattern and attitudes of urban artisans.

6. Explain the major events and message of the Great Awakening, including its comparative impact on new England and the southern colonies and its effects on colonial political life.

Practice in Historical Thinking Skills

After reading this chapter, you should be able to:

1. Compare and contrast the development and maturing of English society in the farming northern colonies, in the plantation South, and in colonial cities.

2. Discuss the foundations of colonial political structures and ideology, including what colonists meant by a political balance of power and how it matched the reality of Whig ideology and local political arrangements.

3. Analyze how the kaleidoscopic mixture of ethnic, racial, religious, and regional settlements in North America, as well as class differences, provided awkward incongruities and threats of social unrest in the various societies of the New World.

(4) ENRICHMENT IDEAS

1. Find and examine other tax lists than the ones in the RTP to see how they reveal inequalities of wealth. Look at (or imagine) the tax records for the citizens of your hometown today to see how they continue to shed light on the distribution of wealth.

2. If you live in the East, you will probably be able to visit a historic house that dates from this period. In the South, see the country houses of the new gentry class or their town houses in Williamsburg. In the North and the Mid-Atlantic states, there are fine old houses of the merchant class and often of German immigrants. What do the houses suggest about daily life and about the class structure of the eighteenth century? Do you see evidences of slaves or servants? What suggestions are there about the lives of women and children? What would you conclude about the nature of work and leisure? Does the historic preservation of a house present a romanticized version of life in the past?

3. Consider recent episodes of religious revivalism. What has changed and what is the same?

4. Does the existence of pluralistic ethnic, racial, religious, and regional groups strengthen or threaten American cultural and political life today?

Instructor:

5. Portraits and artifacts, as well as houses, can be used to provide insights into work and leisure, values and aesthetic standards, class relationships, consumption tastes, family life, and gender roles.

6. America's Families: A Documentary History, edited by Donald Scott and Bernard Wishy, has some wonderfully revealing documents on courtship, love, marriage, parenting, and apprenticeships, which can be made into handouts to stimulate analysis and discussion.

7. As a documentary exercise or as part of a lecture, reproduce for students (and read aloud) portions of Jonathan Edwards's "Sinners in the Hands of an Angry God" in order to discuss the nature and impact of the theology and language of the Great Awakening. Discuss or have students discuss how Edwards's style and theology is different from and similar to that of modern revivalists.

8. Have students evaluate the appeal of Edwards (or George Whitefield) from the perspective of a Puritan or Anglican clergyman, a slave, a farmer, the farmer's wife, a New England merchant, or others. How might they differ? This can lead into a discussion of the relationship of religion to social and political norms.

9. A good slide lecture topic is to show what the architecture of early eighteenth-century churches reveals about the nature of religion.

(5) FURTHER RESOURCES

Documentaries and Films

1. <u>Doorway to the Past</u> (28 mins.; uses archaeology as a means of re-creating eighteenth-century life)

2. <u>Gunsmith of Williamsburg</u> (62 mins.), <u>Silversmith of Williamsburg</u> (44 mins.), <u>Hammerman in Williamsburg</u> (37 mins.; made by colonial Williamsburg, these show artisans at work)

3. <u>Music of Williamsburg</u> (40 mins.; shows an imaginary day at colonial Williamsburg through a light romantic plot and the rendering of several colonial forms of musical expression: sea chanty, black folk song, church chapel music, country fiddling, and an eighteenth-century opera)

4. <u>The Inventory</u> (28 mins.; focuses on the lives of lower middle-class Americans at mid-century)

5. <u>The Chesapeake Planter</u> (28 mins.; uses recreation of a Chesapeake farm to show the way of life of colonial farmers in the Chesapeake region)

Recording

<u>Colony Days</u>, from Oscar Brand's American Folksong Archive

5

Bursting the Colonial Bonds

(1) CHAPTER OUTLINE

Shoemaker Ebenezer MacIntosh finds that the Stamp Act crisis offers him opportunities for influence and prominence. He leads mobs during the Stamp Act crisis protesting against both English authority and Boston's elite.

The Climactic Seven Year's War

    War and the Management of Empire
    Outbreak of Hostilities
    Tribal Strategies
    Consequences of War

The Crisis with England

    Sugar, Currency, and Stamps
    Stamp Act Riots
    An Uncertain Interlude
    The Growing Rift
    The Final Rupture

The Ideology of Revolutionary Republicanism

    A Plot Against Liberty
    Rejecting Monarchy
    Balancing Liberty and Power
    Debate over Political Equality

The Turmoil of Revolutionary Society

    Urban People
    Protesting Farmers

Conclusion: Forging a Revolution

(2) SIGNIFICANT THEMES AND HIGHLIGHTS

1. Beginning with Ebenezer MacIntosh, the chapter stresses the role of common people in the events leading to the American Revolution rather than placing the usual emphasis on famous founding fathers.

2. The chapter shows that there was widespread group support for not one but two American revolutions. As MacIntosh's activities suggest, the "dual American Revolution" combined an external struggle to sever colonial ties to England with an internal struggle for control and reform of colonial society. The colonists sought liberation from English rule. But they also sought to combat the aristocratic, elitist nature of colonial society. The first revolution, marked by violent conflict with England, was the War for American Independence; the second, which involved intense class resentments, is called the American Revolution. The first ended in the Declaration of Independence; the second continued long into the next century.

3. The chapter not only explains these two revolutions but also interweaves colonial history with events in Europe and with the Native American tribes of the interior forests. The perspectives, survival strategies, and cultural changes of the Iroquois, Creek, and Cherokee are seen to be just as important as those of the British, French, and American colonists. The harmful effects of the Seven Years' War loom large in this chapter, especially on groups like the urban laboring poor, backcountry farmers, and women.

4. These groups each had their own struggles against concentrated wealth and power. But these differences were fruitful, for with educated lawyers and rich merchants and planters they fashioned a political ideology of revolutionary republicanism.

(3) LEARNING GOALS

Familiarity with Basic Knowledge

After reading this chapter, you should be able to:

1. Make a clear statement distinguishing between the War for American Independence and the American Revolution.

2. Describe the issues at stake in the series of wars of empire among England, Spain, France, and the several Native American Indian tribes, and outline the major developments and consequences of the Seven Years' War.

3. Outline the steps in the crisis with England between 1763 and 1776 leading to the War for American Independence.

4. Explain the essential issues and elements involved in the ideology of revolutionary republicanism.

5. Describe the grievances and concerns of ordinary Americans between 1763 and 1776, explaining how urban people, women, and farmers understood their "liberties" and "natural rights" in the early 1770s.

Practice in Historical Thinking Skills

After reading this chapter, you should be able to:

1. Discuss the two revolutions going on in the British colonies between 1763 and 1776, explaining the main characteristics of each and indicating which revolution you think motivated the American people more in the 1760s and 1770s.

2. Assess the mutual impact and influence of the interior Native American tribes, the American colonists, and the British and French on one another in the mid-eighteenth century.

3. Identify the chapter author's interpretation of "the nature of the American Revolution" and cite the evidence presented to support that point of view.

(4) ENRICHMENT IDEAS

1. Study again the RTP for this chapter, noting how
    the inventories contribute to your understanding
    of the class tensions and internal social
    struggle that was part of the American
    Revolution.

2. If you live in a rural area or small town (especially
    in the Midwest), it is likely that your local
    newspaper will advertise several auctions of the
    property and household belongings of family farms in
    the process of dissolution. Go to an auction or two,
    and note how the items for sale reflect social class.

3. If you live in the East, you can visit such Revolu-
    tionary sites as Philadelphia, Boston, and Lexington
    and Concord, as well as battle sites at Bunker Hill
    (Breed's Hill), Saratoga, Trenton, Valley Forge,
    Brandywine, and Yorktown. What interpretation is
    provided at these sites? Which "American Revolution"
    is presented? Is there any indication of the social
    tensions of the inner war? How do you explain the
    approach taken at these Revolutionary-era sites?

Instructor:

4. Students can be asked to research and role-play the
    interaction of various groups in pre-Revolutionary
    years: Iroquois and Creek chiefs, British colonial
    officials, backcountry farmers, French fur traders,
    slaves, urban workers, colonial pamphleteers. Divide
    the class into groups representing these various
    interests and perspectives, and ask them to prepare
    position papers on the attitudes, goals,
    strategies, sources of support and power, and the
    like, for each group. Bring them together to hear
    various strategies and tactics for survival and
    success.

5. Your lecture to large classes on the differences
    between the War for American Independence and the
    American Revolution can be dramatically underlined
    for students by arbitrarily assigning each half of
    the lecture hall to one of the two sides of the dual
    American Revolution. Invite each group to think and
    feel itself into the appropriate grievances and
    goals as you talk, interrupting your lecture from
    time to time to direct questions to one side or the
    other to reaffirm the differences. Chapters 8 and 9

in Nash, <u>Retracing the Past</u>, Volume One are pertinent.

6. Films such as <u>The American Revolution</u>, <u>1770-1783: A Conversation with Lord North</u>; <u>Song of Molasses</u> and <u>Cry Riot</u> (about the Sugar and Stamp acts) and <u>The American Revolution: The Cause of Liberty</u> can be used to stimulate a discussion of the English perspective and view of colonial protests as well as the colonists' own view of their grievances. This can be followed by a lecture on the role of violence and mob action in American history.

7. It is often helpful to present the events of the pre-Revolutionary years from the English perspective to show why it was so difficult to resolve difficulties between the colonies and Great Britain. Other than by films, this can be done as a lecture or, if you feel comfortable doing so, by role-playing an English statesman commenting in Parliament on the troubles in the colonies.

8. Give students excerpts from <u>Common Sense</u>, and have them assess the material as political philosophy and as propaganda. Other political documents and statements, such as the resolutions of the Stamp Act Congress, the speeches of Patrick Henry in the Virginia House of Burgesses or of Edmund Burke, the Earl of Chatham, and others in Parliament, and the writings of John Dickinson, Thomas Jefferson, and John Adams also lend themselves well to study and discussion, not only to help students learn the political issues of the Revolutionary era but also to help them learn how to read such documents. Use overheads or handouts in large lecture classes.

9. Above all, students should have an opportunity to read the Declaration of Independence and discuss its meaning and significance. A copy is in the Appendix of the text.

(5) FURTHER RESOURCES

Documentaries and Films

1. <u>Alistair Cooke's America</u>. Episode 3, <u>Making a Revolution</u> (55 mins.)

2. <u>John Adams: Revolutionary (1770-1776)</u>, from <u>The Adams Chronicles</u> (59 mins.; deals with events leading to the calling of the First Continental Congress)

3. <u>Seventeen Seventy-six: Saga of Western Man</u> (52 mins.: re-creates the year by using the words and scenes of the founding fathers)

4. <u>The American Revolution, 1770-1783: A Conversation with Lord North</u> (33 mins.; an engaging imaginary interview with Peter Ustinov as Lord North)

5. <u>The American Revolution: The Cause of Liberty</u> (24 mins.; a series of letters between a patriot and his son, who is studying law in London, as tensions mount in the colonies; the story is continued in <u>The American Revolution: The Impossible War</u>)

6. <u>Song of Molasses</u> and <u>Cry Riot</u> (dramatic re-creations of the American response and outcry over the Sugar and Stamp acts)

Slides

American History Slide Collection, group B ("The Age of the American Revolution")

Recordings

1. <u>Literature of Revolutionary America</u> (readings of documents of the times, including the Declaration of Independence)

2. Wallace House, <u>Ballads of the American Revolution, 1767-1775</u> (Scholastic)

PART TWO

A REVOLUTIONARY PEOPLE
1776–1828

6

A People in Revolution

(1) CHAPTER OUTLINE

"Long Bill" Scott, wounded and captured by the British, explains that the ambition to better himself rather than patriotism led him to join the Revolutionary army. Still, in the next few years, he escapes twice from the British, fights in New York and Rhode Island, and volunteers for the navy. The main effect of the war for Long Bill and his family, however, was not military exploits but poverty, sickness, and death.

The War for American Independence

> Creating an Independent Government
> The War in the North
> The War Moves South
> Native Americans in the Revolution
> The Devastation of the Iroquois
> Negotiating Peace
> The Ingredients of Victory

The Experience of War

> Recruiting an Army
> The Casualties of Conflict
> Civilians and the War
> The Loyalists
> Blacks and the Revolution

The Revolution and the Economy

      The Interruption of Trade
      Boom and Depression in Agriculture
      Manufacturing and Wartime Profits
      Financial Chaos

The Ferment of Revolutionary Politics

      Politicizing the People
      Mobilizing the People
      The Limits of Citizenship
      Republican Women

Revolutionary Politics in the States

      Creating Republican Governments
      Different Paths to the Republican Goal
      Separating Church and State
      Loyalists and Public Safety
      Slavery Under Attack
      Politics and the Economy

Conclusion: The Crucible of Revolution

(2) SIGNIFICANT THEMES AND HIGHLIGHTS

1. As Long Bill Scott's sad but heroic story reveals,
    people in America during the Revolution struggled not
    only to create a nation but even more to improve
    their own lives. This chapter emphasizes the private
    struggles and hardships and the disrupted lives of
    people in America during the Revolutionary War rather
    than the battles and public policy decisions of the
    war. The chapter continues the account of class
    divisions in American society during wartime, which
    underlines the theme of a "dual revolution."

2. This chapter creates a mood that underlines the
    startling facts that the American Revolutionary War
    was the longest war in American history (except one),
    the most costly in per-capita casualties (except
    one), and (without exception) the most damaging in
    terms of per-capita victimization of civilians and
    the disruption and disarray of economic life.

3. It was in state politics that Americans transformed
    and expressed the political meaning of the
    Revolution. The making of new state governments

involved converting the ideology of revolutionary republicanism into action, first by writing state constitutions and second by resolving the thorny issues of Revolutionary times.

4. Although many more ordinary people--white farmers, small shopkeepers, urban artisans, and the like, were politicized and joined the political process, there were limits to republican representation and political participation. Large numbers of Americans-- women, blacks, Native Americans--were excluded from the new political system. This chapter captures their voices as they express their frustrations with a revolution that stopped short of the full realization of its ideological rhetoric.

(3) LEARNING GOALS

Familiarity with Basic Knowledge

After reading this chapter, you should be able to:

1. Describe the major British and American strategies in the American Revolution and state how well they worked.

2. Explain four or five reasons why the Americans defeated the British and won the war.

3. Describe the economic costs of the war to commerce, agriculture, and manufacturing.

4. Explain how the war affected slaves, Loyalists, and Native American Indians, especially the Iroquois.

5. List the questions that the early republican politicians (or anyone, for that matter) asked when thinking about creating new governments.

6. State a few key differences between the Pennsylvania and Massachusetts state constitutions.

7. State the ways in which Americans were politicized in the Revolutionary era.

Practice in Historical Thinking Skills

After reading this chapter, you should be able to:

1. Analyze how the American people made the shift from separating from an imperial system to the creation of a republican form of government.

2. Assess the extent to which the American Revolution, on balance, was good or bad for slaves, northern farmers, Loyalists, Native Americans, wealthy Patriots, and ordinary citizens.

3. Assess how well Americans were able to fulfill their revolutionary republican ideology in the war and the postwar era.

(4) ENRICHMENT IDEAS

1. Explore in the RTP the way in which enlistment and muster rolls reveal the social character of Revolutionary War soldiers. Do you think the poor shouldered an unnecessarily heavy burden of the fighting? Interview some veterans of recent American wars, or find studies of the social-class and racial composition of modern soldiers. What do you conclude?

2. If you live in the East, visit Revolutionary War battle sites at Boston, New York, Trenton, Princeton, Bennington, Saratoga, Brandywine, Savannah, Charleston, Cowpens, Guilford Court House, or Yorktown. Imagine yourself a common soldier at one of those battles. Write a letter home or a diary entry describing what it was like.

3. Imagine you are a former Crown official, or a slave, or a New England farmer, or a northern artisan, or a Virginia Patriot slave owner, or a woman living on the frontier, or some other colonist. What reasons would you give to explain your support for or against the war?

4. Difficult material like political ideology is sometimes easier to understand by representing abstract ideas in some sort of visual way. Construct a chart on revolutionary republican ideology, showing such things as political focus and structures (branches and levels of government), ways of

balancing liberty and power, and ideas about equality and who should rule; for example, a continuum:

```
      LIBERTY                      POWER/ORDER
      ----------------------------------------
      HAPPINESS                    PROPERTY

            the  P E O P L E
```

or a diagram showing John Adams's "Thoughts on Government" and his proposal for the Massachusetts state constitution:

```
      LEGISLATIVE              EXECUTIVE    JUDICIARY

REPRESENTATIVE   SENATE      GOVERNOR
 ASSEMBLY        (Council)   (President)
 .democratic     .aristocratic .independent  .separate
 .the many       .the few      .the one      and
 .liberty        .property     .balancer     distinct
```

Instructor:

5. A discussion of the impact of war on people's lives, as soldiers and as civilians, can be based on items 2 and 3 above and item 15 in section 3. You could divide students into small groups and assign each one either a battle or a Revolutionary-era person, asking each group to develop either a battle description or a person's position on the war. There is more on "Long Bill" Scott in Chapter 11 of Nash, Retracing the Past, Volume One.

6. Films are of course useful in larger classes. The American Revolution: The Impossible War follows the Laurens family during wartime. It neglects the home front, however, and students can critique the film for its overemphasis on the military struggle. If students were to make a film about the Revolution, ask what they would emphasize and include.

7. Jay Fliegelman, in Prodigals and Pilgrims: The American Revolution Against Patriarchal Authority, 1750-1800, shows that the Revolution was not only a rejection of English authority but a rejection of patriarchal authority in general. The book suggests intriguing linkages between social and political change and could lead to a stimulating lecture and discussion.

(5) FURTHER RESOURCES

Documentaries and Films

1. Black Winter (deals with varying motivations and commitments to the struggle)

2. The American Revolution, 1770-1783: A Conversation with Lord North (33 mins.; Eric Sevareid interviews Lord North, played by Peter Ustinov)

3. The Other Side of Victory (a common soldier's experiences during the American Revolution)

4. Private Yankee Doodle (28 min.; focuses on common soldier and features a military reenactment)

Slides and Filmstrips

1. American History Slide Collection, group B

2. Five filmstrips, The Revolution, from the American Heritage Media Collection

Recordings

1. Revolutionary War, audiocassette from Oscar Brand's American Folksong Archive

2. Richard Bales, The American Revolution: A Cantata Based on the Music of the American Colonies During the Years 1775-1800 (Columbia Records)

3. Wallace House, Ballads of the American Revolution, 1776-1781 (Scholastic)

7

Consolidating the Revolution

(1) CHAPTER OUTLINE

Timothy Bloodworth of New Hanover County, North Carolina, rises from humble origins and gains a substantial position in his community and the respect of his neighbors. Although he becomes a delegate to the Confederation Congress in 1784, he soon loses confidence in the Articles of Confederation and supports the call for a special convention to meet in Philadelphia in 1787. When he views the constitution that emerges from that convention, however, he fears that the gains of the Revolution will be lost. He works tirelessly to defeat the new proposal. As a result of his efforts and the efforts of men like him, North Carolina only endorsed the new union when the Congress had forwarded a national bill of rights to the state for its approval.

Struggling with the Peacetime Agenda

> Demobilizing the Army
> Opening the West
> Wrestling with the National Debt
> Surviving in a Hostile World

Political Tumult in the States

> The Limits of Republican Experimentation
> Shay's Rebellion

Toward A New National Government

    The Rise of Federalism
    The Grand Convention
    Federalists Versus Anti-Federalists
    The Struggle for Ratification
    The Social Geography of Ratification

Conclusion: Completing the Revolution

(2) SIGNIFICANT THEMES AND HIGHLIGHTS

1. As the anecdote of Timothy Bloodworth suggests, this chapter explores the uncertain world facing Americans after the Revolutionary War had ended. Many feared the new government would not be able to assure settlement of the country's interior or pay off the massive war debt. The new nation was a weak newcomer in a world still dominated by powers like Great Britain.

2. The frantic pace of political experimentation on the state level moderated after 1783 as conservative arrangements replaced some of the radical ones passed only a few years earlier. As Shay's Rebellion suggested, however, many had not forgotten the cries for equal rights and popular consent that had been so powerfully expressed in 1776.

3. This chapter presents the political controversies marking the writing and ratification of the Constitution and explains the struggle for ratification of that document.

(3) LEARNING GOALS

Familiarity with Basic Knowledge

After reading this chapter, you should be able to:

1. Describe the terms of the land ordinances of 1785 and 1787 and the ideas behind the conquest theory.

2. Itemize the steps taken by Robert Morris to deal with the national debt.

3. Explain the causes and consequences of Shay's Rebellion.

4. Describe the reasons for dissatisfaction with the Articles of Confederation.

5. State the major compromises worked out at the Constitutional Convention and the major features of the original Constitution--its organizational format and the most significant allocations of power, rights, and responsibilities.

6. Outline the major arguments of Federalists and Anti-Federalists in the debates over ratification of the Constitution.

Practice with Historical Thinking Skills

After reading this chapter, you should be able to:

1. Explain the reasons for the success of the Federalists in writing and securing the ratification of the Constitution.

2. Analyze how the Constitution changed and strengthened the government that had existed under the Articles of Confederation.

3. Describe the different political and social perspectives of the Federalists and Anti-Federalists.

(4) ENRICHMENT IDEAS

1. Find an Indian treaty for the Native Americans in your region and discover what it suggests about the attitudes and values of both the white and Native American treaty-makers.

2. The complete text of the United States Constitution is found in the appendix of <u>The American People</u>. Read and study the Constitution, breaking it down into its major parts, and identify the five or so most significant points to remember in each part.

3. Make a chart contrasting the major differences between the Declaration of Independence and the Constitution over their primary purposes, the quality and style of language, political ideology, assumptions about human nature and ends of government, and how to achieve political change.

Instructor:

3. After working through the RTP on Indian Treaties,
    engage the students in a discussion of treaty-making
    with Indians as a reflection of both cultural
    differences and the foreign policy of an exuberant
    new nation.

4. Create your own diagram of republican ideology as a
    handout or blackboard presentation as the basis for a
    lecture or discussion (see Chapter 5 Enrichment Idea
    number 4).

5. Have students role-play a Massachusetts town meeting
    in 1779 as the citizens meet to decide whether to
    select two delegates to the state constitutional
    convention and to instruct them on such issues as the
    structure of government, the rights of the people,
    land and money policy, and how far to extend
    political rights. Break the class into such groups
    as landed Patriot elite, yeoman "middling" farmers,
    town artisans, lawyers and other professionals,
    landed Loyalist elite, blacks, women, and "riffraff."
    See Robert Gross's Minutemen and Their World (New
    York: Hill & Wang, 1976) for further ideas. The
    instructor should serve as moderator of the meeting
    and bring a large gavel.

6. Students can be asked to consider their own process
    of politicization (development of political awareness
    and belief) and to discuss how this was similar to or
    different from that of eighteenth-century Americans.
    In large lecture classes, students can share their
    thoughts with those sitting next to them first, and
    then the instructor can solicit a sampling of
    experiences from the class.

7. Reenact the Constitutional Convention by assigning
    students roles as delegates from particular states
    and perspectives and asking them to prepare and
    present arguments in their own words for the kind of
    constitution they wanted.

(5) FURTHER RESOURCES

Documentaries and Films

1. <u>Constitution: One Nation.</u> parts 1 and 2 (30 mins. each; arguments pro and con and ratification are covered)

2. <u>The Constitution: The Compromise That Made a Nation</u> (27 mins.; dramatic reenactment of the debates over representation in the Constitutional Convention)

8

Creating a Nation

(1) Chapter Outline

David Brown, Revolutionary War veteran, seaman, and pamphleteer, increasingly attacked the central government under the new national constitution in the 1790s. He claimed it was a conspiracy of the rich to exploit farmers, artisans, and other common folk. His inflammatory charges aroused the ire of the federal judiciary, which convicted him of sedition and put him in prison. He was released only after the election of Thomas Jefferson in 1800.

Launching the National Republic

> Launching the New Government
> The People Divide
> The Whiskey Rebellion

The Republic in a Threatening World

> The Promise and Peril of the
> French Revolution
> Citizen Genet and the Democratic-Republican
> Societies
> Jay's Controversial Treaty

Federalists Versus Jeffersonians

> The Election of 1796

War Crisis with France
Alien and Sedition Acts
Local Reverberations
The "Revolution of 1800"

Conclusion: Toward the Nineteenth Century

(2) SIGNIFICANT THEMES AND HIGHLIGHTS

1. As David Brown's story suggests, this chapter
   presents the turbulent political controversies
   surrounding launching of the new government in the
   1790s.

2. The struggle to create a nation was marked by the
   formation of two political parties, Federalists and
   Democratic-Republicans, and by crises in the young
   nation's relationships with France and England
   during the presidential administrations of George
   Washington and John Adams.

3. Underlying the political controversies of the 1790s,
   as David Brown's life reveals, were class differences
   between rich and poor, regional differences between
   the urban Northeast and the interior West and South,
   and two conflicting ideological views over issues of
   power, political equality, and the proper role of
   central government in a republican society.

(3) LEARNING GOALS

Familiarity with Basic Knowledge

After reading this chapter, you should be able to:

1. Describe the Bill of Rights.

2. Outline Hamilton's view of the proper role of
   government, his financial plan, and the fate of each
   proposal.

3. State the major events of George Washington's
   administration, including the causes of the Whiskey
   Rebellion.

4. State how the French Revolution divided Americans and
   contributed to the development of party politics.

5. Describe the social composition, political
    principles, and activities of the
    Democratic-Republican societies.

6. Describe the major domestic and foreign crises of the
    administration of John Adams.

Practice in Historical Thinking Skills

After reading this chapter, you should be able to:

1. Discuss the disagreement over the role of government
    in the new nation.

2. Compare and contrast the differing ideological
    positions and visions of the Federalists and the
    Democratic-Republicans in the 1790s.

3. Decide whether the election of 1800 was, as Jefferson
    thought, "a revolution in the principles of our
    government."

(4) ENRICHMENT IDEAS

1. After examining the paintings in the RTP and opening
    for this chapter, look up and study other patriotic
    paintings of the Revolutionary era by John Barralot,
    John Trumbull, Gilbert Stuart, Charles Willson Peale,
    and others. What kind of mythology do they depict
    about the founding fathers? What kinds of
    mythologies exist today about American heroes? Are
    our heroes still political figures? If not, who are
    they? What does the choice of a nation's heroes
    suggest about that nation's values?

2. Make a chart contrasting the major ideas, political
    principles, and social composition of the two
    emerging political party traditions.

Instructor:

3. Ask the students to read and analyze some of the
    best-known Federalist Papers (Nos. 10, 51, and 78,
    for example) analyzing them line by line and
    paragraph by paragraph in order to learn how to read
    important political documents from the time of the
    nation's founding. Other crucial documents could
    include Washington's Farewell Address, the letters to

Washington by Hamilton and Jefferson on the national bank, and Jefferson's Inaugural Address in 1801. In large lecture classes this can be done with an overhead projection of the text.

4. Although many believe that George Washington was mythologized in the nineteenth century, the process actually began in the Revolutionary period, as a study of graphics suggests. As part of item 1, you could discuss the process of mythologizing national heroes. Wendy Wick's <u>George Washington: An American Icon</u> has 101 prints, some of which could be reproduced for students to study for themselves or made into slides for a lecture.

5. Ask students to research and prepare speeches presenting the major ideological views of prominent Federalists and Republicans on one of the key issues of the 1790s: Hamilton's financial plan, the French Revolution, Jay's Treaty, the unofficial war with France, or the Alien and Sedition Acts.

6. Lecture or discussion topics include the differing ideological views of Federalists and Republicans on the issues mentioned in item 7 and Fisher Ames's question prompted by the Whiskey Rebellion: Can the rulers in a democracy employ physical force in order to maintain what they think is a threat to domestic order and tranquility without turning the moral force of public opinion against government? The question has importance both for the 1790s and the 1980s. See Chapter 14 in Nash, <u>Retracing the Past</u>, Volume One.

(5) FURTHER RESOURCES

Documentaries and Films

1. <u>Alistair Cooke's America</u>. Episode 4, <u>Inventing a Nation</u> (55 mins.)

2. <u>John Adams President (1797-1801),</u> (59 mins.; from <u>The Adams Chronicles.</u>)

9

Politics and Society in the Early Republic

(1) CHAPTER OUTLINE

Handsome Lake, a Seneca Indian, fashions a message of renewal and hope for his people. His revival draws from Native American traditions as well as from the values and ideas of white culture. The revitalization that Handsome Lake promotes is only one of the strategies Native American tribes pursue in the early decades of the nineteenth century.

Restoring Republican Liberty

The Jeffersonian Republicans Take Control
Cleansing the Government
The Judiciary and the Principle of Judicial Review
Dismantling the Federal War Program

Building an Agrarian Republic

The Jeffersonian Vision
The Windfall Louisiana Purchase
Exploring and Opening the Trans-Mississippi West

Indian-White Relations in the Early Republic

Land and Trade
Civilizing a "Savage" People
Strategies of Survival: The Cherokee

Patterns of Armed Resistance: The Shawnee
and the Creek

A Foreign Policy for the Agrarian Republic

Jeffersonian Principles
Struggling for Neutral Rights
The War of 1812
The United States and the Americas

Culture and Politics in Transition

The Tensions of Republican Culture
Politics in Transition
The Specter of Sectionalism
A New Style of Politics
Collapse of the Federalist-Jeffersonian Party

Conclusion: The Passing of an Era

(2) SIGNIFICANT THEMES AND HIGHLIGHTS

1. This chapter focuses on the first three decades of
the nineteenth century, a period of intense political
activity and westward expansion. The chapter
emphasizes the attempts of the Jeffersonian
Republicans to reshape national political life and to
realize their vision of liberty in an agrarian
republic.

2. As the anecdote of Handsome Lake suggests, the chapter continues the story of Indian-white relations.
Between 1790 and 1820, tribal groups developed
strategies of resistance and survival. Some tribes,
like the Seneca whom Handsome Lake inspired,
underwent cultural renewal. Others, like the
Cherokee, adopted many of the ways of white society.
Still others, like the Shawnee and Creek nations,
chose armed resistance. At the same time, federal
policies were developed, based on both humanitarian
and territorial concerns, that would guide
Indian-white relations for the rest of the
nineteenth century.

3. In the field of foreign affairs, Jeffersonians
attempted to fashion policies that would free the
nation of entangling alliances with European powers,
eliminate foreign troops from American soil, and
protect American maritime interests. Although

foreign policy measures were in the short run
unsuccessful, as the War of 1812 indicated, the
United States soon stated its unique claim to the
Western   Hemisphere.

4. Efforts to create a distinctive American culture
    faltered because of disagreements over the value of
    the country's English heritage and because of the
    association of culture with social class.

(3) LEARNING GOALS OF THIS CHAPTER

Familiarity with Basic Knowledge

After reading this chapter, you should be able to:

1. Explain three measures Jefferson took to reshape and
    cleanse the federal government.

2. List the main functions of the federal government in
    the early nineteenth century.

3. Explain the reasons why Jefferson believed agricul-
    tural life was essential to political liberty.

4. Show how changing land acts affected settlement of
    the public domain.

5. Show the conflicting goals of federal Indian policy.

6. Outline the causes and significance of the War of
    1812 and of the Monroe Doctrine.

Practice in Historical Thinking Skills

After reading this chapter, you should be able to:

1. Compare and contrast the survival strategies of the
    Cherokee, Shawnee, and Creek nations and evaluate how
    well you think their different strategies worked.

2. Discuss the validity of the American claim that the
    War of 1812 was the "second War of American
    Independence."

3. Explain the forces that weakened Jefferson's party.

(4) ENRICHMENT IDEAS

1. Do the imaginary map exercise described in the RTP
    for this chapter. Then turn to an actual outline map
    of the United States and trace the route of the Lewis
    and Clark expedition. Fill in the area acquired in
    the Louisiana Purchase and trace the Transcontinental
    Treaty Line of 1819 (Adams-Onis). What conclusions do
    you draw about the relationship between exploration
    and expansion? Finally, add Florida, New Orleans,
    and other important battle sites of the War of 1812.

2. Develop a position paper supporting or rejecting war
    with Great Britain from the point of view of a member
    of Congress from the South, the West, and New
    England. What would be the differences between the
    positions and specific arguments of the three
    congressmen?

3. In the library, look at some of the volumes on
    American art. What materials are included from the
    period covered by this chapter? What has the author
    said about the art? What are your observations? Do
    they correspond to the views of American culture
    suggested in the concluding section of this chapter?

Instructor:

4. A lecture (with maps) on geography is appropriate for
    this chapter. Contemporary students do not work
    enough with maps, and this is an opportunity to show
    the influence of geography on history.

5. Give students a copy of the Cherokee constitution and
    have them study it to analyze the extent to which the
    Cherokee had adopted the values of white society and
    to what extent they preserved traditional Cherokee
    culture. See Chapter 18 in Nash, <u>Retracing the Past</u>,
    Volume One.

6. Have students examine the participation of women in
    the Second Great Awakening (see Nancy Cott's article
    in <u>Feminist Studies</u> 3, 1975). Students could also
    analyze hymns as a way of seeing changing religious
    views, comparing the hymns to earlier religious
    documents. These ideas lend themselves readily to
    the lecture format.

7. The Monroe Doctrine is a significant and lasting
    landmark document, suitable for an exercise in the

analysis of a document. Students can examine the text not only for what it says explicitly about other nations but also for what it implies about the differences between the United States and other nations and the role of the United States in the Western Hemisphere.

(5) FURTHER RESOURCES

Documentaries and Films

1. <u>John Quincy Adams: Secretary of State, 1817-1825</u> (59 mins.)

2. <u>John Quincy Adams: President, 1825-1829</u> (59 mins.)

3. <u>Alistair Cooke's America</u>. <u>Episode 6, Firebell in the Night</u> (52 mins.; emphasizes signs of sectional division)

4. Two films from the series <u>Equal Justice Under the Law</u> deal with judicial landmarks: <u>Marbury v. Madison</u> (33 mins.) and <u>McCulloch v. Maryland</u> (35 mins.)

10

The Preindustrial Republic

(1) CHAPTER OUTLINE

Ben Thompson and Phyllis Sherman, former slaves, come to New York to join its free black community. Although they benefit only marginally from the city's economic opportunities and not at all from its supposed opportunities for social equality, they carve out a life for themselves among other free blacks.

The Preindustrial Economy

The Return of Commercial Prosperity
Agriculture in the North
The South Embraces Cotton
Preindustrial Manufacturing
Merchant Capitalism and the Putting Out System
Panic and Depression
An Ideology of Expectant Capitalism

The Nature of Preindustrial Society

A Nation of Regions
A Nation of Communities
Lives of Intimacy and Quietness
Lives of Difficulty and Trial
Birth, Death, and Disease
Patterns of Wealth and Poverty

Perfecting Republican Society

The Youthfulness of America
The Meaning of Social Equality
The Doctrine of Individualism
The Second Great Awakening and Social Reform
Alleviating Poverty and Distress
Educating the Republic's Children
Women in Republican Society
The Limits of Reform: Race and Slavery

Conclusion: Between Two Worlds

(2) SIGNIFICANT THEMES AND HIGHLIGHTS

1. This chapter surveys American life between 1790 and 1820 and characterizes the period as one poised between old ways of life and new ones. It shows the continuities with the past--the dependence on overseas trade, the traditional rhythms of agricultural life, and the dominance of small-scale production, along with signs of change--commercial expansion, the rise of merchant capitalism, the birth of the cotton kingdom and the early textile industry, and changing modes of transportation.

2. The description of the local and personal character of preindustrial life and society includes regional differences in class systems and the troubling growth of poverty. Americans led lives that were "intimate and quiet" as well as rigorous and difficult.

3. The chapter explains the ideological underpinnings for changing attitudes toward economic growth and social equality as well as the ambivalent ways in which Americans attacked their social problems in the republican experiment.

(3) LEARNING GOALS

Familiarity with Basic Knowledge

After reading this chapter, you should be able to:

1. List three reasons for the prosperity of the 1790s.

2. Explain why America's economic status can be described as neocolonial.

3. Show three changes in northern agriculture in the early nineteenth century and give four reasons for its limited productivity.

4. Explain the impact of the cotton gin on southern agriculture and show how cotton reinforced the institution of slavery.

5. Name three groups of Americans who were conspicuous among the nation's poor.

6. Explain why Americans were increasingly interested in reform.

Practice in Historical Thinking Skills

After reading this chapter, you should be able to:

1. Explain why Americans embraced capitalism in the early nineteenth century.

2. Describe the most striking aspects of early nineteenth-century communities and analyze the ways in which they were changing.

3. Explain the arguments that could be made in 1815 both to support the institution of slavery and to argue for its dissolution.

(4) ENRICHMENT IDEAS

1. Using the data on Ohio from the census returns of 1820 in the RTP for this chapter, construct as full a picture as you can of family and household life in the early nineteenth century. What would these (or similar) counties look like today? How have family and household structures changed in the more than 165

years since 1820, and how do you account for these changes?

2. There are several living-history farms and museum villages that seek to capture daily life in the period covered by this chapter. If you are located near Sturbridge Village in Massachusetts, Turkey Run Farm Park in Virginia, or another early nineteenth-century restored village, make sure you visit them. What continuities do you see with life in the past? What signs of change? How accurately does the site interpretation convey the picture of life described in this chapter? If you were in charge of revising the interpretive program, what changes might you suggest?

3. Imagine yourself as either Ben Thompson or Phyllis Sherman, the two free blacks featured in the anecdote. How might they compare their lives in New York with the lives they had led in Maryland and Connecticut? Make a list of the benefits and disadvantages of living in New York for free blacks.

4. Think of what you might write in a daily journal if you lived in a northern agricultural community, on a cotton plantation, in a port city, or on the frontier. What kinds of activities might you mention? In what ways would your life be one of "intimacy and quietness"? What might be your worries and concerns?

5. Historic houses dating from this period are to be found in many parts of the country. A visit to a house museum or a walking tour of older sections of an eastern city will reveal much about living standards, class structure, convenience, and comfort.

Instructor:

6. Ample material on the changes in shoe production in Lynn (by Alan Dawley and Paul Faler) can provide the basis for a lecture on the significance of merchant capitalism, the changing lives of artisan workers and their families, and the transformation of work. Reference to the Cary budget will help students understand much about daily life.

7. Letters and diaries of young women from the 1790s and early 1800s can be used to provoke a discussion of the changes and continuities in the lives of American middle-class women.

8. The film <u>Turkey Run Farm Park,</u> although it has some intrusive comparisons between the past and the present, can be used as the basis for a discussion of the chapter themes.

9. A lecture or discussion based on the significance of drinking and disease in the past can illustrate some of the hazards of urban life in the early nineteenth century.

10. Students can focus on the Burke-Crady affair discussed in this chapter. Ask them to work out the main points of a newspaper appraisal of the "trial" given to the two immigrants. Some students can be instructed to support the decision and others to criticize it.

(5) FURTHER RESOURCES

Documentaries and Films

1. <u>Turkey Run Farm Park</u> (24 mins.)

2. <u>Before the Industrial Revolution</u> (17 mins.; shows eighteenth- and nineteenth-century trades in rural America)

3. <u>Had You Lived Then: Life in 1800</u> (16 mins.; filmed in Cooperstown, New York, and made for younger audiences, this film nevertheless does a good job of showing daily life around 1800 and some of the currents of change)

Filmstrips

<u>The First Frontiers,</u> from the American Heritage Media Collection

PART THREE

AN EXPANDING PEOPLE
1820–1877

11

Currents of Change in the Northeast and the Old Northwest

(1) CHAPTER OUTLINE

Mary Paul works in the Lowell mills as a young girl of 15 and finds her situation exhilarating. Over the next few years, however, she discovers some of the disadvantages of mill work. Like many Americans, she finds economic change brings both new opportunities and new uncertainties.

Economic Growth

Components of Growth
Immigration
Transportation: The Critical Factor
Capital Investment
The Role of Government
The Innovative Mentality
Ambivalence Toward Change
The Advance of Industrialization

The Manufacturing World

The Impact of Industrialization
A New England Textile Town
Working and Living in a Mill Town
Female Responses to Work
The Changing Character of the Work Force
Factories on the Frontier

The Urban World

> The Process of Urbanization
> Class Structure in the Cities
> The Urban Working Class
> Middle-Class Life and Ideals
> Mounting Urban Tensions
> The Black Underclass

Rural Communities

> Farming in the East
> Frontier Families
> Opportunities in the Old Northwest

Conclusion: The Character of Progress

(2) SIGNIFICANT THEMES AND HIGHLIGHTS

1. This chapter, as Mary Paul's experience suggests, concentrates on the economic and social transformations in the Northeast and the Midwest between 1820 and 1860. The chapter discusses the factors contributing to economic growth, particularly the importance of changes in transportation, and explores industrialization as a new means of production and as a source of social change. The chapter shows that the process of industrialization was uneven, as old and new ways of production existed side by side.

2. Five types of communities (Lowell; Philadelphia; Cincinnati; Hampshire County, Massachusetts; and the Indiana frontier) are discussed to show how each participated in economic growth. The ways in which various classes, ethnic groups, and races responded to new conditions and shared or failed to share in the benefits of growth are highlighted.

3. The persistence of Revolutionary ideology is evident in working-class critiques of the new industrial world, while new middle-class ideals emerged as a response to changing economic and social conditions.

4. Samuel Breck and Joseph Sill, both of Philadelphia, are introduced as examples of upper- and middle-class urban dwellers. Several mill girls (Mary Paul and Sally Rice) appear at various points in the chapter. The Skinners give an idea of life on the Indiana frontier.

(3) LEARNING GOALS

Familiarity with Basic Knowledge

After reading this chapter, you should be able to:

1. List several factors contributing to economic growth and explain how changes in transportation were of critical importance.

2. Define the term <u>industrialization</u> and identify the parts of the United States where industrialization took hold between 1830 and 1860.

3. Define the <u>cult of domesticity</u> and explain the reasons for its development and describe new views of childhood.

4. Describe urban class structure and compare it to rural class structure.

5. Explain the process of establishing a family farm on the midwestern frontier.

6. Discuss the contribution of nontangible factors to economic growth.

Practice in Historical Thinking Skills

After reading this chapter, you should be able to:

1. Show how Cincinnati illustrates the uneven process of industrialization and the emergence of new types of work and new workers and contrast the situation in Cincinnati with the Lowell system.

2. Analyze the ways in which both male and female workers used Revolutionary ideology as a means of criticizing the new work order.

3. Summarize the ways in which economic and social changes affected people's lives both by increasing opportunities and benefits and by separating people from one another.

(4) ENRICHMENT IDEAS

1. Using the RTP as your guide, explore some volumes of early nineteenth-century paintings. What can you discover about the nature of daily life, attitudes, and values from your study?

2. Think how you might write an article for a Cincinnati newspaper evaluating some of the changes in work in the antebellum period if you were the owner of a furniture factory, a widow taking in piecework, or a former cabinetmaker now working in the factory.

3. Write a diary entry for one day in the life of a Lowell mill girl in the 1830s. Give a clear sense of your daily schedule as well as your response to your job and free time. How would your entry differ if you were an Irish girl in the 1850s?

4. If you live in the Midwest, visit the Conner Prairie Settlement near Indianapolis. This living-history museum, which uses first-person interpreters as villagers, conveys a realistic picture of daily life on the frontier in the 1830s. Other living museums can suggest the ways in which rural American life changed in the period before the Civil War.

5. If you live in or near a northeastern or Middle Atlantic city, plan a walking tour to the part of the city constructed during the period covered by this chapter. What kinds of buildings date from that era? What were they used for? Are there any examples of housing? What class of persons may have lived in these houses? Are there any remaining evidences of working-class neighborhoods? Visit an early mill complex. What can it tell you about the industrial process, the nature of work, and the reality of life in a mill community?

Instructor:

6. Using the sections in the chapter on working-class protest in Cincinnati, Lowell, and Philadelphia as background, elaborate on the working-class critique of industrialization, the rise of working men's parties, and similar topics.

7. Edward Pessen has studied the emerging patterns of urban inequality in several cities. This can provide a basis for a lecture on or discussion of the relationship between economic growth and American

class structure. The _Lowell Offering_ provides the upbeat side of mill work.

8. Some of the documents and songs coming from strikes and other protests can provide the basis for analysis and discussion and show the ways in which Revolutionary ideology was adapted to meet changing economic conditions.

9. Make a slide presentation on the nature of middle-class life, including housing and artifacts, urban life, mill life, or whatever else your slide library or your own collection suggests. This presentation can be a lecture, or students can be encouraged to analyze the slides themselves for what they reveal about social life in the early nineteenth century.

10. Stories and illustrations from _Godey's Lady's Book_ can be used as a starting point for a discussion of changing middle-class norms. The work of Linda Gordon and James Mohr on contraception can be linked to changing demographic patterns and new notions of family life--an intriguing topic for a lecture.

(5) FURTHER RESOURCES

Documentaries and Films

1. _American Folk Art_ (25 mins.; covers eighteenth and nineteenth centuries up to the Civil War)

2. _Pictures to Serve the American People: American Lithography, 1830-1855_ (22 mins.)

3. _Under the Cover: American Quilts_ (11 mins.; shows the skills of American women)

4. _Anonymous Was a Woman_ (30 mins.; folk art created by American women in the eighteenth and nineteenth centuries)

Recordings

Rivers and Lakes, audiocassette from Oscar Brand's American Folksong Archive

12

Slavery and the Old South

(1) CHAPTER OUTLINE

Frederick Douglass learns from his masters about complex, intricate chains that bind slaves and masters to each other. He also learns that education is the way to freedom.

Building the Cotton Kingdom

>   Economic Expansion
>   White and Black Migrations
>   The Dependence on Slavery
>   Slavery and Class in the South
>   The Nonslaveholding South

Morning: Master in the Big House

>   The Burdens of Slaveholding
>   Justifying Slavery

Noon: Slaves in House and Fields

>   Daily Toil
>   Slave Health
>   Slave Law and the Family

Night: Slaves in Their Quarters

> Black Christianity
> The Power of Song
> The Enduring Family

Resistance and Freedom

> Forms of Black Protest
> Slave Revolts
> Free Blacks: Becoming One's Own Master

Conclusion: Douglass's Dream of Freedom

(2) SIGNIFICANT THEMES AND HIGHLIGHTS

1. The tremendous growth of agriculture in the Old South was dependent on cotton and slavery. But contrary to myth, the South was an area of great diversity, regionally, socially, and in terms of class and slave ownership. These differences bred tensions among whites as well as between masters and slaves.

2. Although slavery was a labor system, the chapter emphasizes the daily life and complex, entangled relationships of white masters and black slaves and points out the difficulties of generalizing about their relationships. The experiences of the family of rice planter Robert Allston suggests some of the dimensions of white slaveholders' lives, while the youth of Frederick Douglass illuminates the lives of black slaves.

3. A unique structure in this chapter discusses slavery in three sections: morning in the Big House, which focuses on white masters; noon in the fields, which looks at daily work and other hardships of the slaves; and nighttime in the quarters, which describes a slave culture and community centered around religion, music, the family, and other adaptive survivals from African culture.

4. Racism was not confined to the South but existed throughout American society. Racism as well as slavery limited black freedom. To a much lesser extent, southern slaveholders also suffered limitations on their freedom from the burdens of the slave system.

(3) LEARNING GOALS

Familiarity with Basic Knowledge

After reading this chapter, you should be able to:

1. Distinguish several geographic regions and describe the socioeconomic class variations of slaveholding patterns in the Old South.

2. Describe the burdens of slavery from the perspective of the slaveholders and explain five ways in which they justified slavery.

3. Describe a typical day on the plantation for slave men and women, both in the house and in the fields.

4. Explain the nature of black family life and culture in the slave quarters, including how religion, music, and folklore gave the slaves a sense of identity and self-esteem.

5. List five ways in which the slaves protested and resisted their situation.

Practice in Historical Thinking Skills

After reading this chapter, you should be able to:

1. Develop arguments for and against slavery from the perspective of southern slaveholders, nonslaveholding southerners, northern whites, slaves, and freed blacks.

2. Discuss and evaluate the question of who was "free" in southern antebellum society.

3. Identify the author's interpretation of slavery and other possible interpretations.

(4) ENRICHMENT IDEAS

1. Find more folktales and stories told by slaves and analyze what they reveal about slave culture. See Harold Courlander, A Treasury of Afro-American Folklore (1976) or J. Mason Brewer, American Negro Folklore (1968).

2. Listen to some slave spirituals and work songs and analyze them. What do they reveal about the slave

experience and about attitudes toward religion?
Notice the double meanings. See Chapter 20 in Nash,
Retracing the Past, Volume One.

3. Are there any historical sites in your area related
    to slavery--for example, plantations, stations on the
    underground railroad, or slave markets? Do restored
    plantations give a balanced view of life on the old
    plantation, the slave quarters as well as the Big
    House?

4. Consider the heritage of slavery in modern society.
    To what extent does it still affect our lives and
    how?

5. Are blacks and whites more or less "free" today than
    they were during slavery? Are they more or less
    entangled with each other?

Instructor:

6. Read some folktales together in class and lecture on
    or discuss the kinds of questions raised in the RTP
    for this chapter about folktales. Play some
    spirituals in class and discuss them (as in item 2).
    Discuss the recording of Malcolm X's "Message to the
    Grass Roots" (side 2), where he talks about house and
    field slaves.

7. Other lecture or discussion topics: Compare slavery
    with the "wage slavery" of northern workers. Compare
    the degrees and types of racism in the antebellum
    South and North. Explore the question, Who is free
    when slaves and masters are bound to each other?

8. Slavery presents a good opportunity for a
    historiographic lecture helping students to
    understand different schools of interpreting slavery:
    apologist and neoapologist (U. B. Phillips, Genovese,
    Fogel and Engerman), abolitionist (Stampp, Elkins),
    and black perspective (Blassingame, Rawick, Gutman,
    Raboteau).

9. Role-play several scenes from plantation life
    featuring difficult decisions. Examples: Two slaves
    discuss whether to run away. Two slaves try to
    decide whether to get married or to have children. A
    master with financial problems talks with a friend
    (or his wife) about whether to sell a favorite
    slave. A master and overseer consider the punishment
    of a runaway slave--what form the punishment should
    take and possible consequences.

Students can construct in writing the pros and cons for each situation ahead of time, or they can act out the scenes with only a few minutes to think about their role in class. An interesting (and powerful) way to conclude some of the scenes is to bring the master and slave together for a second scene after resolution of the first one. Remember to spend time afterward debriefing--talking about the role play, and how characters felt, and what they learned.

10. Students are usually engaged by a lecture or discussion on the various effects of slavery and racism on women, the wives of plantation owners as well as slave women. See Elizabeth Fox--Genovese, <u>Within the Plantation Household: Black and White Women of the Old South</u>.

(5) FURTHER RESOURCES

Documentaries and Films

1. <u>Roots</u>. Episode 7, <u>Uprooted</u> (50 mins.; deals with black family and sexual exploitation of slave women)

2. <u>Slavery</u> (30 mins.; uses spirituals and testimony of the slaves)

Slides

   <u>American History Slide Collection,</u> group H

Recordings

   Your favorite recording of black spirituals

13

Shaping America in The Antebellum Age

(1) CHAPTER OUTLINE

Emily and Marius Robinson are separated shortly after their marriage because of their ardent commitment to abolish slavery and to educate free blacks. Despite suffering many hardships of separation, sickness, and mob attack, they persist for a time in an effort to shape and reform American society.

The Political Response to Change

    Changing Political Culture
    Jackson's Path to the White House
    Old Hickory's Vigorous Presidency
    Jackson's Bank War and "Van Ruin's" Depression
    The Second American Party System

Religious Revival and Reform

    Finney and the Second Great Awakening
    Reform and Politics
    The Transcendentalists

Utopian Communitarianism

    Oneida and the Shakers
    Other Utopias
    Millerites and Mormons

Reforming Society

    Temperance
    Health and Sexuality
    Humanizing the Asylum
    Working-Class Reform

Abolitionism and Women's Rights

    Tensions Within Antislavery
    Flood Tide of Abolitionism
    Women's Rights

Conclusion: Perfecting America

(2) SIGNIFICANT THEMES AND HIGHLIGHTS

1. The social and economic changes of the 1830s were both promising and unsettling. This chapter explores the question of how people (both ordinary and prominent) sought to maintain some sense of control over their lives in the 1830s and 1840s. Some, like the Robinsons, poured their energies into reform. Others turned to politics, religion, and new communal life styles in order to shape their changing world.

2. Throughout the chapter social, political, cultural, and economic phenomena are interrelated and seen as a whole. The chapter merges two major events-- democratic Jacksonian politics and the many forms of perfectionist social reform. They began from distinctly different points of view but in fact shared more in common than has usually been recognized.

3. The explanation of politics in the age of Jackson looks at the social and ethnocultural basis of politics, while the analysis of revivalism, religion, and utopian communitarianism stresses the socioeconomic basis of these cultural phenomena.

4. The timeless dilemmas and problems of reformers, especially of temperance, abolitionist, and feminist reformers, is a sub-theme running through the chapter.

(3) LEARNING GOALS

Familiarity with Basic Knowledge

After reading this chapter, you should be able to:

1. Describe three ways in which political culture changed between the early 1820s and 1840.

2. Explain the course of events of the three major issues in Jackson's presidency--the tariff, the war against the bank, and Indian removal.

3. List and explain the leaders, principles, programs, and sources of support of the two major parties, Democrats and Whigs.

4. List several evils that Americans wanted to reform in the 1830s and 1840s and the major influences that contributed to the reform impulse.

5. Describe some of the purposes, patterns, and problems that most utopian communities shared.

6. Describe the major goals, tactics, and problems in the antebellum reform movements for temperance, abolitionism, and women's rights.

Practice in Historical Thinking Skills

After reading this chapter, you should be able to:

1. Analyze how Jacksonian politicians and social reformers both opposed one another and had much in common.

2. Explain the development of the second American party system, showing how it evolved from and differed from the first party system.

3. Explain and understand why people turn to politics, or to religion and revivalism, or to utopian communitarianism, or to specific issue reforms in order to shape their world; and then explain how well these seemed to work.

(4) ENRICHMENT IDEAS

1. After working through the RTP, consider other foreign visitors' accounts of life in the United States in the 1830s and 1840s. How accurate are they? How would you write about another culture you have seen (or imagined)? What questions would you ask? What limitations would you feel? What cultural assumptions would you bring to your observations?

2. Visit the site of one of the several utopian communities mentioned in the chapter. Many still exist, some even restored as living historical museums. Depending on where you live, you might visit Hopedale or Brook Farm near Boston; Shaker villages near Pittsfield, Massachusetts and in Kentucky; Ephrata, Pennsylvania; Zoar, Ohio; New Harmony, Indiana; the Amana colonies in Iowa, etc. Whether or not you can actually visit the original site, you can study one or two particular utopian communities.

3. Imagine yourself as part of the colony. How well would you fit in? What would you like and dislike about life in this community? Write a letter to a friend about it, or write a series of imaginary diary entries about life in the community.

4. You can think about similar questions when visiting other sites, for example, Seneca Falls, or Mormon landmarks in Utah, or a prison asylum built in the mid-nineteenth century. A letter or diary entry could be written about your imagined participation in a Whig campaign picnic in 1840, or a revival or temperance meeting broken up by a mob, or a meeting of Mormons considering migration westward, or your presence at the women's rights convention in Seneca Falls.

5. Prepare a diagram showing the development of the American political party system from the 1790s to 1840--specifically party names, leaders, principles, programs, campaign issues, and sources of popular electoral support.

Instructor:

6. Divide the class into groups and ask each to plan a utopian community. What rules, principles, policies and purposes would they want in this community? What

problems do they anticipate? Have students present their work to the class, and then discuss which community sounds most appealing and why.

7. The 1830s and 1840s was a period rich in powerful rhetoric, both oral and written. Using overheads (for large classes) or handouts (depending on your duplication budget), class time can be well spent analyzing and discussing documents. For example, Jackson's bank veto message, selections from the Webster-Hayne debate or Calhoun's <u>Exposition and Protest,</u> a Finney revival sermon, Garrison's first issue of <u>The Liberator</u> and Douglass's first issue of the <u>North Star</u>, selections from Sarah Grimke's <u>Letter on the Equality of the Sexes</u>, the Seneca Falls "Declaration of Sentiments", and the exchange of letters between Theodore Weld and Angelina Grimke or between Marius and Emily Robinson.

8. A lecture on one or two utopian communities and the solutions they offered to the perceived problems of the age can be drawn from the rich literature on utopianism. The lecture could end (or begin) with a short comparison to the communal movement of the 1960s and 1970s or even to students' experiences in their living units.

(5) FURTHER RESOURCES

Documentaries and Films

1. <u>John Quincy Adams: Congressman (1830-1848)</u>, (55 mins.; from <u>The Adams Chronicles</u>)

2. <u>New Harmony: An Example and a Beacon</u> (29 mins.)

3. <u>Working for the Lord</u> (53 mins.; religious communes)

14

Moving West

(1) CHAPTER OUTLINE

Lewis Cass presents an optimistic picture of what the westward movement represented for the nation. The experiences of Henry Judah and Thomas Gibson in the Mexican War suggest the underside of westward expansion, as do Mary Gibson's worried letters to her husband.

Probing the Trans-Mississippi West

> Foreign Claims and Possessions
> Traders, Trappers, and Cotton Farmers
> Manifest Destiny

Winning the Trans-Mississippi West

> Annexing Texas
> War with Mexico
> California and New Mexico
> The Treaty of Guadalupe Hidalgo
> The Oregon Question

Going West

> The Emigrants
> Migrants' Motives
> The Overland Trails

Living on the Frontier

    The Agricultural Frontier
    The Mining Frontier
    The Mormon Frontier
    The Urban Frontier

Cultures in Conflict

    Confronting the Plains Tribes
    The Fort Laramie Council
    Overwhelming the Mexicans

Conclusion: Fruits of Manifest Destiny

(2) SIGNIFICANT THEMES AND HIGHLIGHTS

1. As the contrasting views of Lewis Cass, Henry Judah, and the Gibsons make clear, the story of the trans-Mississippi West in the nineteenth century is not just the story of the acquisition of territory but also of the experience of thousands of ordinary citizens who fought for new lands or who migrated to the frontier.

2. The chapter emphasizes the use of personal documents, especially the diaries written by men and women on the Overland Trail, in reconstructing historical realities.

3. The political and military events that led to the successful acquisition of western lands came at the expense of Native Americans and Mexicans. The events of this period are presented not only through the eyes of white emigrants but also from the perspective of these two groups.

4. Lewis Cass's attitudes and ideas exemplify the point of view and rhetoric of expansionists who advocated the acquisition of new territories.

(3) LEARNING GOALS

Familiarity with Basic Knowledge

After reading this chapter, you should be able to:

1. Define Manifest Destiny.

2. List the sequence of events resulting in the acquisition of Texas, New Mexico, California, and Oregon and locate on a map and date the major territorial acquisitions of the United States between 1803 and 1853.

3. Describe the typical emigrant and three motives leading to the decision to migrate to the Far West.

4. List four ways in which white emigration affected the livelihood of Plains Indians.

5. Explain the terms of the Laramie Council agreements and assess their impact on red-white relations.

6. Contrast the experience of Mexican-Americans in Texas, New Mexico, and California.

Practice in Historical Thinking Skills

After reading this chapter you should be able to:

1. Discuss the United States's policies toward the Plains Indians, placing those events in the context of Indian-white relations until the early 1850s.

2. Compare and contrast opportunities on the mining and farming frontiers.

3. Analyze the role of men and women on the Overland Trail.

(4) ENRICHMENT IDEAS

1. The RTP gives examples of diaries and personal documents written on the Overland Trail and suggests that men and women differed in the content and style of what they wrote in their diaries and journals. Many diaries have been collected and published. Read some of them. What seem to be the typical daily

concerns of men? Of women? What can you conclude
about the nature of trail life? What work was
involved in moving west? What can you learn about
family and social life through the diaries? Finally,
do you find differences between journals written by
men and those written by women? How do you connect
these materials with the cult of domesticity and the
idea of separate spheres for men and women?

2. The letters of many of the young men who participated
    in the gold rush are found in printed collections.
    Some may also be on file with your local historical
    society, as the men wrote letters to friends and
    family at home. What picture of mining life can you
    form from these personal documents? How much
    opportunity was there in the mining West as reflected
    in these letters? Did the writers have reasonable
    expectations of their future? What can you tell
    about family life and the social character of mining
    life through reading the letters?

3. In some parts of the United States (Alaska, the
    West), a later frontier period is still fresh in the
    memories of older residents. This provides an
    excellent opportunity for an oral history.

4. On an outline map of the United States, draw in and
    date the major territorial acquisitions between 1803
    and 1853 and the major overland trails and important
    junctions.

Instructor:

5. This chapter provides another good opportunity to
    work on students' knowledge of geography, especially
    of the West. The chapter also provides a chance to
    talk about land, wilderness, environmentalism, and
    ecology and to raise questions about the appropriate
    use of land and resources. The third edition of
    Roderick Nash's Wilderness and the American Mind and
    his readings book on The American Environment will
    provide material for lectures and discussion.

6. Students can write and present arguments supporting
    or opposing the annexation of Texas in 1844, the
    declaration of war against Mexico in 1846, or the
    ratification of the Treaty of Guadalupe Hidalgo in
    1848. Their positions can provide the basis for
    either a role-play debate or a conventional discus-
    sion.

7. Emigration songs, paintings, and slides or other visual materials are good departure points for a slide lecture on popular images of the West, of Native Americans, of motivations for emigration and who went west, of men and women on the frontier and what their experiences were like, and of attitudes toward the wilderness. Four fascinating paintings filled with images worth discussing are Thomas Cole's five-part sequence The Course of Empire (1830s), George Caleb Bingham's The Emigration of Daniel Boone (1852), Emanuel Leutze's Westward the Course of Empire Takes Its Way (1861), and John Gast's Westward-Ho (Manifest Destiny) (1872).

8. A study of views of the West in popular culture (movies, novels, television) can also provide the basis for a slide presentation, lecture, or discussion on "cowboys and Indians," Chicanos, frontier women, the wilderness, and other issues that raise the question of the relationship between popular images, myths, and realities in history.

9. The Turner thesis can be used for either a lecture or a class discussion to explore the issue of opportunity in the American West and the characteristics of the American character. Begin with an anecdote drawn from letters and diaries by frontier women or gold miners.

10. Students might be asked to consider how the materials in this chapter might be relevant to the situation of Chicanos and Native Americans today, the longevity of the ideas of Manifest Destiny in terms of American foreign policy, or the significance of the pioneer heritage.

(5) FURTHER RESOURCES

Documentaries and Films

1. Alistair Cooke's America. Episode 5, Gone West (55 mins.)

2. Catlin and the Indians (25 mins.; illustrates Plains Indian life through Catlin's paintings)

3. Folk Songs of Western Settlement, 1787-1853 (14 mins.)

82

4. <u>The West of the Imagination</u> (six VHS/Beta programs, 52 mins. each; focusing on the western experience and its impact on the American imagination, especially art)

Slides and Photographs

1. <u>American History Slide Collection,</u> groups C, J, and P

2. Paintings by Thomas Cole, Albert Bierstadt, Frederick Church, George Catlin, Frederic Remington, George Caleb Bingham, and other painters of the American West

3. <u>The California Gold Rush</u> (18 photos) and <u>The War with Mexico, 1846-1848</u> (14 photos), available from Documentary Photo Aids

Recordings

<u>Westward Movement,</u> audiocassette from Oscar Brand's American Folksong Archive

15

The Union in Peril

Northern Views and Visions
The Southern Perspective

Polarization and the Road to War

The Dred Scott Case
Douglas and the Democrats
Lincoln and the Illinois Debates
John Brown's Raid
The Election of 1860

The Divided House Falls

Secession and Uncertainty
Lincoln and Fort Sumter

Conclusion: The "Irrepressible Conflict"

(2) SIGNIFICANT THEMES AND HIGHLIGHTS

1. The heightened tensions surrounding the 1860 election
    and suggested by the anecdote indicate the central
    place the Civil War occupies in American history.
    The causes of the war that dissolved the Union,
    therefore, are crucial to an understanding of
    America's history. The causes reflect the
    interrelationship of politics, emotions, and
    sectional culture.

2. Historians have long debated, without resolution, the
    causes of the Civil War. This chapter focuses on
    four developments of the period between 1848 and
    1861, each an important cause of war. The chapter
    weaves these developments together in an interpretive
    narrative account of both the events and the cultural
    values behind the events. The student is left to
    decide how the four causes interacted to bring about
    the war and which, if any, were more important than
    others.

3. Events in Kansas in 1855 and 1856 are highlighted as
    a specific microscopic illustration bringing together
    many of the forces that led Americans to secession
    and civil war in 1861.

4. The primary focus in this chapter is on national
    political developments involving nationally known
figures because the Civil War was, after all,

fundamentally a political event. Nevertheless, the
    chapter includes the comments of ordinary Americans,
    most frequently those of two figures from earlier
    chapters, runaway slave Frederick Douglass and South
    Carolina rice planter Robert Allston, as they
    observed the events of the 1850s leading to the
    outbreak of civil war.

(3) LEARNING GOALS

Familiarity with Basic Knowledge

After reading this chapter, you should be able to:

1. Explain three or four proposals for dealing with the
    territories acquired in the Mexican War and the
    five provisions of the Compromise of 1850.

2. Describe the breakdown of political parties in the
    early 1850s, explaining the disappearance of old
    parties and the emergence of new ones.

3. Outline the course of the Kansas-Nebraska Act and how
    it affected politics and sectional animosities in the
    mid-1850s.

4. Explain America's expansionist interest in Latin
    America.

5. Show how the events in Kansas in 1855 and 1856, the
    Dred Scott case, the emotional events of 1859-1860,
    and the election of Lincoln led to the secession
    crisis and the outbreak of the Civil War.

Practice in Historical Thinking Skills

After reading this chapter, you should be able to:

1. Describe the differing cultural values of the South
    and North and each section's view of the other, and
    explain how these cultural differences helped lead to
    civil war.

2. Explain the development and significance of each of
    the four causes of the Civil War, citing four or five
    specific examples for each.

3.   Evaluate the four causes, indicating which ones (or
     one) you think were most significant in explaining
     why the North and South went to war in 1861.

                  (4) ENRICHMENT IDEAS

1.   RTP: Read further into the Senate debates over the
     Compromise of 1850, analyzing and discussing the
     style and arguments of various speeches, especially
     the complete texts of those by Clay, Webster,
     Calhoun, and Seward.

2.   It is 1855. Create a dialogue between two recent
     migrants to Kansas, one from Massachusetts and one
     from Missouri. Put them in an appropriate setting
     and provide an end to their conversation, but focus
     mainly on how each reveals his or her sectional
     origins and views and how each sees the other.

3.   You are Lincoln in the winter of 1860-1861. What
     would you do? You are Frederick Douglass in the same
     winter. What would you do? You are Robert Allston
     at the same time. What would you do? Why? What do
     you think would happen?

Instructor:

4.   Have students read, analyze, and discuss the
     speeches by Lincoln and Douglas during their debates
     in Illinois in 1858. Have them reenact one of the
     debates in class, including the postdebate arguments
     that went on in various local taverns over which
     candidate had made the better case. See Chapter 25
     in Nash, Retracing the Past, Volume One.

5.   Reenact the election of 1860. Students representing
     individual candidates can prepare campaign strategies
     and speeches. Conclude with a mock election in which
     students should be able to state which candidate
     they voted for and why. Some students can serve as
     political analysts commenting on the campaign and the
     significance of the election results.

6.   The causes of the Civil War suggest a lecture on
     historical causation (and interpretive
     historiographic points of view), explaining to
     students the differences between the fundamental,
     underlying, root causes of a major historical

phenomenon and the precipitating events that sparked it.

7. Either of the two visual presentations listed under Further Resources will provide a thoughtful context for the enrichment suggestions in this section, especially as a backdrop for staging or discussing the Lincoln-Douglas debates or the election of 1860.

8. The organization of this chapter into four sections, each treating one of the four major causes of the Civil War, provides a good opportunity to show students (in a lecture) how to organize and structure important major topics in American history as well as how to outline chapters in preparation for the final examination.

(5) FURTHER RESOURCES

Films and Filmstrips

1. <u>Alistair Cooke's America</u>. Episode 6, <u>A Firebell in the Night</u> (55 mins.)

2. <u>Voices of Blue and Gray: The Civil War</u> (Guidance Associates) is a three-part filmstrip done in 1973 with a script by Thomas Frazier (including poignant quotes from primary sources such as diaries, newspaper editorials, personal letters, and political speeches), comprised of <u>Slavery</u> (15 mins.), <u>The War</u> (17 mins.), and <u>The Aftermath</u> (17 mins.)

16

The Union Severed

(1) CHAPTER OUTLINE

A young northern man, Arthur Carpenter, begs his parents for permission to join the army and wins their consent. A southern Presbyterian preacher, George Eagleton of Tennessee, feels compelled to enlist and leaves his sorrowful wife, Ethie, and their baby to go to war.

Organizing to Fight the War

> The Balance of Resources
> The Border States
> Challenges of War
> Lincoln and Davis

Clashing on the Battlefield, 1861-1862

> War in the East
> War in the West
> Naval Warfare
> Cotton Diplomacy
> Common Problems, Novel Solutions
> Political Dissension

The Tide Turns, 1863-1865

> The Emancipation Proclamation
> Unanticipated Consequences of War

Changing Military Strategies

Changes Wrought by War

      A New South
      The Victorious North
      On the Home Front
      Wartime Race Relations
      Women and the War
      The Election of 1864
      Why the North Won
      The Costs of War
      An Uncertain Future

Conclusion: Union Triumphant

(2) SIGNIFICANT THEMES AND HIGHLIGHTS

1.   This chapter attempts to provide a coherent picture of the Civil War as a military and diplomatic event, but, as the stories of Arthur Carpenter and the Eagletons suggest, the chapter emphasizes the impact of the war on the lives of ordinary people: soldiers who fought the war and noncombatants behind the lines, such as women like Ethie Eagleton and Emily Harris, slaves, and working-class Americans.

2.   In numerous, unanticipated ways, the war transformed northern and southern society. The changes were most dramatic in the South, where by the war's end leaders were contemplating the use of slaves as soldiers and even emancipation. Ironically, although the war was fought to save distinctly different ways of life, the conflict forced both sides to adopt similar measures and to become more alike.

3.   In the North, the war was fought to save the Union. Only gradually did goals shift to include the emancipation of slaves. Lincoln's racial leadership is emphasized despite his inability to reduce racism significantly in northern society.

4.   The chapter continually shows the contrasts between northern and southern resources, leadership, military strategy, wartime political and economic problems and solutions, and the impact of the war on race relations, women, daily life, and other features of the home front.

(3) LEARNING GOALS

Familiarity with Basic Knowledge

After reading this chapter, you should be able to:

1. Compare and contrast the balance of resources in the North and the South at the war's beginning and its end.

2. State the significance of the border states to both the Union and the Confederacy.

3. List the various manpower and financial measures taken by the Confederate and Union governments during the course of the war.

4. Describe the origins, purposes, and provisions of the Emancipation Proclamation.

5. List the ways in which Lincoln and Davis expanded presidential powers.

6. Describe the participation of women in the war.

Practice in Historical Thinking Skills

After reading this chapter, you should be able to:

1. Discuss the social political and economic impact of the war on both societies and show how the South became increasingly similar to the North.

2. Analyze the impact of the Emancipation Proclamation on the course of the war and on race relations.

3. Analyze why the North won the war and the South lost it.

(4) ENRICHMENT IDEAS

1. Study a volume of photographs of the Civil War taken by Mathew Brady and others. Choose two or three photographs and study them closely. First, describe what they contain: What objects are in each? What people? How are they dressed? What are their expressions (faces and bodies)? What appears to be the relation between them? Then draw some

conclusions: What atmosphere has been created? Why were the photos taken and for whom? What can you learn about the Civil War by studying photos of the conflict? What are the limitations of this kind of historical evidence? How has the technological level of the equipment shaped photography?

2. Find some letters or diaries written by a participant in the Civil War. You may have some in your family, or check your college or university library archives; most historical societies will have manuscript resources of this kind. If all else fails, there are good published collections of letters and diaries written by soldiers. You might also want to look at materials written by people at home. What kinds of experience does your writer describe? What seems important to him or her? What understanding of the war does your writer have?

3. If a Civil War battlefield is nearby, visit it. Imagine yourself a typical soldier writing home with news of that battle. What would you say?

Instructor:

4. Use a personal document such as a diary or some letters as the basis of a class discussion on the points mentioned in items 1-3. Or use the document to provide personal interest for a lecture.

5. Have students read Michael Shaara's The Killer Angels, a novel about the battle of Gettysburg, as the basis of a discussion.

6. Ask the students to review the chapter and, in groups, to decide what they might want to include or emphasize if they were to make a film on the Civil War. Showing the film Some of the Boys (34 mins.), which focuses on life in the ranks, could provide the basis for a more extended discussion.

7. Divide the students into groups. Give each group the task of developing the main points for an editorial evaluating the leadership of either Lincoln or Davis in 1864. If each group is given a distinct political position, there can be a lively discussion of each of the leaders when the groups report on their editorial.

8. Lecture topics include extending the chapter's points about the importance of political leadership, Lincoln's racial views, the unintended changes that occurred in the North and South during the war, and the argument that the war was a rich man's war but a poor man's fight.

9. Have the class listen to records of Civil War songs (cited in section 5) composed by Henry Clay Work, George Frederick Root, and others, and analyze the lyrics and mood conveyed by these songs. How do such songs compare with contemporary popular songs in revealing attitudes about war and other social and political events?

(5) FURTHER RESOURCES

Documentaries and Films

1. Fellow Citizen, A. Lincoln (30 mins.; award-winning film using Lincoln's writings, photographs, and prints

2. True Story of the Civil War (33 mins.; based on photographs by Brady, Jackson, and others)

3. Homefront (30 mins.; also uses Brady photographs)

4. Antietam (56 mins.; historian William Brown focuses on this battle and the experience of the ordinary soldier.

Slides and Filmstrips

1. American History Slide Collection, group D

2. Voices of Blue and Gray: The Civil War, part 2

Recordings

1. Songs of the Civil War (New World Records)

2. Songs of the North and South, 1861-1865 (Columbia)

3. Who Shall Rule This American Nation? Songs of the Civil War Era, by Henry Clay Work (Nonesuch)

4. Richard Bales, The Confederacy and The Union, a two-part cantata based on the music of the South and North during the Civil War years (Columbia)

17

The Union Reconstructed

(1) CHAPTER OUTLINE

Adele and Elizabeth Allston fearfully return to their plantations after the war. At Nightingale Hall, they have a joyous reunion with their former slaves. But at Guendalos, the blacks are defiant, the atmosphere threatening. The morning after the arrival, however, Uncle Jacob, the former black driver, hands the keys to the crop barns over to the women in recognition that they still own the land.

The Bittersweet Aftermath of War

      The United States in 1865
      Hopes Among Freedmen
      The White South's Fearful Response

National Reconstruction

      The Presidential Plan
      Congressional Reconstruction
      The President Impeached
      Congressional Moderation
      Women and the Reconstruction Amendments

Life After Slavery

The Freedmen's Bureau
Economic Freedom by Degrees
Black Self-Help Institutions

Reconstruction in the States

Republican Rule
Violence and "Redemption"
Reconstruction, Northern Style
The End of Reconstruction

Conclusion: A Mixed Legacy

(2) SIGNIFICANT THEMES AND HIGHLIGHTS

1. The account of the Allstons' return to their plantations highlights the focus of this chapter. The primary action of the chapter takes place on the old southern plantation and in the freedmen's cabins, not in the halls of Congress and the White House. Rather than emphasizing the political programs and conflicts of Congress and the president, we see the hopes and fears of ordinary persons--both black and white--as they faced their postwar world. Political events, North as well as South in the years between 1865 and 1877, are included, but they are secondary to the psychosocial dynamics of reconstructing new relationships among differing people after the Civil War.

2. As reflected in the opening anecdote, the dreams and aspirations of three groups--white southerners, black freedmen, and white northerners--are introduced and woven together throughout the chapter. The main question of the chapter is, What happens as these three sets of goals come into conflict? Uncle Jacob's return of the keys to the crop barns to the Allston family, a gesture symbolic of ownership, indicates the crucial importance of labor and land to an understanding of the outcome of these conflicting goals. The result was a mixed legacy of human gains and losses.

3. The experiences of the Allston family are concluded in this chapter. Frederick Douglass's astute observations as a black leader continue as those of W. E. B. Du Bois begin.

4. The tragic elements of the Reconstruction, or any other era, are perhaps best represented in literature. Novels and short stories are used in this chapter to capture these human conflicts.

(3) LEARNING GOALS

Familiarity with Basic Knowledge

After reading this chapter, you should be able to:

1. State four or five particular goals of three groups at the end of the Civil War: the freedmen, white southerners, and white northerners.

2. Describe the situation and mood of the country at the end of the Civil War and describe the first programs and actions of southern whites and freedmen as they redefined race relations in 1865.

3. Explain President Johnson's reconstruction program and contrast it with Congress's alternative program.

4. Name and explain three important acts and three constitutional amendments that were part of the Republican reconstruction program.

5. Explain the arrangements for working the land that developed between white landowners and the freedmen and describe the terms of a typical work contract.

6. Describe the character of the Republican state governments in the South during Reconstruction: Who ruled? How well? For how long? How did these governments come to an end?

Practice in Historical Thinking Skills

After reading this chapter, you should be able to:

1. Assess the relationship between the character of national politics during Grant's term of office from 1869 to 1877 and the end of Reconstruction in the South.

2. Show how the diverse goals of the white southerners, freedmen, and white northerners came into conflict

and assess to what extent each group achieved its various goals by the end of Reconstruction.

3. Evaluate the respective roles southern and northern whites played in impeding black goals.

(4) ENRICHMENT IDEAS

1. The RTP, which focuses on the ways in which novels reflect history, includes only a very brief excerpt from two novels about Reconstruction. Consider in a longer excerpt the style and point of view of the authors of the six novels listed below. Which do you think most accurately reflects the historical truth about Reconstruction? Is the most accurate novel-as-history necessarily the best as literature? Based on these excerpts, which novel do you think you would like to read in its entirety, and why?

    Thomas Dixon,   The Clansman
    Albion Tourgee,   A Fool's Errand
    Howard Fast,   Freedom Road
    W. E. B. Du Bois, Quest of the Silver Fleece
    John De Forest,   Miss Ravenal's Conversion from
                       Secession to Loyalty
    Earnest Gaines,   The Autobiography of Miss Jane
                       Pittman

2. Complete the textbook chart "Conflicting Goals During Reconstruction" for the following groups in 1865 by showing what happened to each group by 1877. How well were each of their earlier goals fulfilled? When you have completed the chart, you are in a position to assess the success of Reconstruction and to understand developments in the South into the twentieth century.

    a. victorious northern radical Republicans
    b. northern moderates (Republicans and Democrats)
    c. old southern planter aristocracy (ex-Confederates)
    d. New "Other South" yeoman farmers and Unionists
    e. black freedmen

3. Write a short story or a series of letters or diary entries describing the typical daily experiences of various persons during Reconstruction. For example, a southern woman, Adele Allston, or her daughter

97

Elizabeth, presiding over a large cotton plantation in the absence of their husband and father who was killed in the war. Or a black family that had been given 40 acres of confiscated land by a northern general during the war and faced a title dispute with and dispossession by the original landowner afterward. Or a poor white family putting their lives together in the changing economic climate and race relationships of the postwar years. Or a Yankee schoolteacher's experiences in a Freedmen's Bureau school in Tennessee. Or a Freedmen's Bureau agent's hectic, overworked, underappreciated daily duties in Mississippi. Read in class and discuss. Notice the clash of unresolved dreams.

Instructor:

4. The first enrichment idea on novels makes a nice extra reading and paper assignment for students.

5. Role-playing Reconstruction: Create three groups representing southern whites, freedmen, and northerners (or six groups, including subcategories of each of the three). Each group should brainstorm together and then write out (1) its goals and dreams, in priority order of importance; (2) its degree of commitment and sources of support; and (3) its methods of attaining the goals. Bring the whole class together to interact around these three assignments, to negotiate, state methods and countermoves, reassess commitments and sources of support, and the like, and arrive at an outcome. Challenge each group to achieve its goals, and discuss at the end what happened: Did each succeed? Why not? Professors, of course, will use their creativity in adapting this idea to their own particular situations.

6. Show on an overhead or hand out a typical freedmen's contract--either for annual labor or for sharecropping or tenancy. (Good examples can be found in Ransom and Sutch, One Kind of Freedom, 1977). Either read through and discuss them with the class, or act out a scene in which you are the land owner going over contracts with freedmen on your land. Break students into groups to decide whether they want to sign the contract and what clauses they might try to renegotiate. These questions can be put to a large lecture class as a whole or by asking three students sitting next to each other to discuss their reactions to the contracts.

7. Show either one or both films, <u>Birth of a Nation</u> and <u>Gone With the Wind.</u> Afterward, discuss their historical validity, the attitudes that informed and sustained their popularity, and why they have become classic American films. Assess their impact on racial attitudes in this century. Then show the final segment of <u>Roots</u> and compare its validity and impact on racial attitudes.

8. The songs of Reconstruction reflect the mood, attitudes, and goals of various groups. Listen to and discuss the full lyrics of freedmen's jubilee songs ("The Master Gone, Ha Ha, the Darkies Stay, Ho Ho"), the unreconstructed Confederate songs ("I'm a Good Old Rebel"), and northern Republican songs ("Who Shall Rule This American Nation?").

(5) FURTHER RESOURCES

Films and Filmstrips

1. <u>The Century Next Door</u> (25 mins.; uses paintings to show daily life in 1870)

2. <u>Voices of Blue and Gray,</u> part 3

Recordings

1. <u>Who Shall Rule This American Nation? Songs of the Civil War Era,</u> by Henry Clay Work (Nonesuch)

2. <u>Folk Songs in American History</u>. Set 2, "Reconstruction at the West"

PART FOUR

AN INDUSTRIALIZING PEOPLE
1865-1900

18

The Farmer's World

(1) CHAPTER OUTLINE

Hattie and Milton Leeper work to establish themselves on the Nebraska frontier. They win a modest prosperity before Hattie dies in childbirth and Milton leaves the family claim. The Ebbesen's, a Danish family, face natural disasters, but they survive and establish themselves in some comfort in a Nebraska town.

Modernizing Agriculture

> Rural Myth and Reality
> New Farmers, New Farms
> Overproduction and Falling Prices
> Farming on the Western Plains: 1880s-1890s
> The Early Cattle Frontier: 1860-1890
> Cornucopia on the Pacific

The Second Great Removal

> Background to Hostilities
> The White Perspective
> The Tribal View
> The Dawes Act: 1887
> The Ghost Dance: An Indian Renewal Ritual

The New South

> Postwar Southerners Face the Future
> The Other Side of Progress
> Cotton Still King
> The Nadir of Black Life
> Diverging Black Responses

Farm Protest

> The Grange in the 1860s and 1870s
> The Interstate Commerce Act: 1887
> The Southern Farmers' Alliance in the 1880s and
> 1890s
> The Ocala Platform: 1890
> The People's Party: 1892

Conclusion: Farming in the Industrial Age

(2) SIGNIFICANT THEMES AND HIGHLIGHTS

1. This chapter focuses on rural America, where, like
    the Leepers and Ebbesens, the majority of Americans
    lived between 1865 and 1900. The chapter shows the
    economic changes of the post-Civil War period:
    Machinery became increasingly necessary, farm
    operations brought new lands into use, and regional
    diversification and crop specialization came to
    characterize American agriculture. The chapter shows
    the impact of these changes on American farmers and
    stresses the significance of falling prices and
    overproduction.

2. The theme of racial conflict on the Plains frontier
    continues from the perspective of both white
    Americans and Native Americans. Black Elk, an
    Ogalala Sioux holy man, provides an example of the
    Native American perspective as the reservation policy
    reaches maturity.

3. The chapter explores the meaning of the "New South,"
    contrasting the reality of northern control, the
    continuing dominance of cotton, and widespread
    poverty with the dreams and goals of New South
    spokesmen. The hardening of racial attitudes in the
    New South is described along with black reactions.

4. Farm protest movements (the Grange and the Southern
    Farmers' Alliance) are explained as responses to new

conditions, although not always entirely rational ones. The interest in collective solutions in the Southern Alliance suggests a link with the labor protest described in Chapter 19. Although the rural discontent is highlighted here, the majority of rural Americans did not participate in overt protest movements.

(3) LEARNING GOALS OF THIS CHAPTER

Familiarity with Basic Knowledge

After reading this chapter, you should be able to:

1. List four ways in which farmers responded to the new conditions of the post-Civil War period.

2. Describe three ways in which the development of the Plains frontier was linked to technological advances.

3. Identify the steps leading to the Dawes Act and describe its terms.

4. Explain the goals of New South spokesmen and contrast the realities of industrial and agricultural development with these goals.

5. Describe the steps stripping blacks of their political rights and the implementation of "Jim Crow" laws, and outline the various black responses.

6. List the major planks of the Ocala Platform in 1890 and of the Omaha Platform in 1892.

Practice in Historical Thinking Skills

After reading this chapter, you should be able to:

1. Discuss the ways in which the Southern Farmers' Alliance represented a more comprehensive approach to the problems of the American farmer than that developed by the Grange.

2. Explain why the 1890s has been called the nadir of black status in the South.

3. Discuss the importance of populism in terms of rural protest and political debate.

(4) ENRICHMENT IDEAS

1. The RTP for this chapter deals with middle-class journals published in the nineteenth century. College and university libraries often have at least some of these journals in their collections. See what your library has. You might want to look through the issues for one of the years discussed in this chapter. What seem to be the major topics of interest in the journals you have chosen? What are the controversial issues? Do the journals deal with any of the events covered here? If so, what are the main points of the discussion? The point of view? Is there much sympathy for the problems of farmers, Indians, or blacks? There are many questions that you might want to ask, depending on your source.

2. Although the film Heartland presents the frontier in a slightly later period, it is worth seeing for the picture it gives of frontier life and in particular a woman's response to frontier conditions. The film is available on videotape.

3. Many novels and books of general interest deal with some of the topics of this chapter--in particular, life on the Plains frontier and the struggle between the Plains Indians and whites. Examples of vivid novels are Hamlin Garland, Main-Travelled Roads (1891); Frank Norris, The Octopus (1901); Willa Cather, O Pioneers! (1913); and Ole Rolvaag, Giants in the Earth (1927). They present many different points of view that you will want to consider.

4. Letters and diaries written by foreign immigrants on the Plains frontier can be found in published form and in local historical societies. They offer an interesting perspective on the frontier experience. Older residents of communities in this region of the country still remember information on frontier life from relatives and family. You could interview some of these residents.

Instructor:

5. A class discussion based on photographic evidence of life on the Plains frontier and a comparison of this frontier (as portrayed by photographers) to earlier frontiers in the Far West can bring out the importance of the environment in shaping life. Letters and diaries offer further insights into frontier

conditions and illuminate the importance of ethnic groups in settling the West. You can build a lecture around these sources as well, using handouts as a way for students in large classes to follow the analysis of various primary visual and written sources.

6. A lecture devoted to the conflict with the Plains Indians could show both Anglo-American attitudes and policies toward Native Americans and the ways in which the post-Civil War clash was related to the modernization of American life.

7. Students can study the lyrics of several songs from the Populist Songbook (see Lawrence Goodwyn) and what the songs reveal about populist positions, appeal, mentality (have students pay careful attention to the choice of words), and popularity.

8. Divide students into groups of poor white farmers in the Midwest, poor white farmers in the South, black sharecroppers in the South, and any other group you think appropriate. Ask the groups to list five of their dreams or goals--they should be as specific as possible. Then have them describe the reality of their situation. Finally, have them determine, given the probable gap between dreams and reality, what they should do. Report and discuss. See Chapters 2, 6, and 7 in Volume Two of Gary Nash, editor, Retracing the Past.

9. Topics that could be expanded into lectures or parts of lecture include an analysis of the Homestead Act and its impact on the settlement of the frontier, a detailed analysis of the evolution of policy toward Native Americans, and a class based on the much-debated question, Who were the populists?

10. A debate between Booker T. Washington and W. E. B. Du Bois on the "Atlanta Compromise" speech can reveal the many fundamental differences between the two leaders. Even a large lecture class can be divided in half, assigning one of the two positions to each half and inviting arguments from both sides.

(5) FURTHER RESOURCES

Documentaries and Films

1. Alistair Cooke's America. Episode 7, Domesticating a Wilderness (55 mins.)

2. End of the Trail (54 mins.; photographs document the subjugation of the Plains Indians)

3. People of the Buffalo (13 mins.; paintings and photos show the role of the buffalo in the life and culture of the Plains Indians)

4. The Americans: Chief Crazy Horse (26 mins.; narrated by Chief White Eagle, focuses on Sioux leader Crazy Horse)

5. The Americans: Geronimo (25 mins.)

6. The Americans: Chief Joseph (23 mins.)

7. Great Grand Mother: A History and Celebration of Prairie Women (29 mins.; the Canadian prairie experience)

8. The Legacy of Currier & Ives (23 mins.; nostalgic view of America shown in prints)

9. The Ballad of the Iron Horse (30 mins; the growth of the railroad and the nation)

10. Red Sunday: The Story of the Battle of the Little Big Horn (28 mins; a prizewinning film focusing on historical forces and the role of personality in the struggle)

11. Ethnic Notions (56 mins; all video formats. Award winning documentary made in 1987 that traces the emergence of racial stereotypes from the 1820s to the modern Civil Rights movement

Slides and Photographs

1. American History Slide Collection, groups C, E, and K

2. The Indians of the Plains (46 photos) and The Real Cowboys (20 photos), available from Documentary Photo Aids

Recordings

1. <u>Authentic Music of the American Indian</u>, three records

2. <u>Loggers and Miners and Cowboy Songs,</u> audiocassettes
   from Oscar Brand's American Folksong Archive

19

The Rise of Smokestack America

(1) CHAPTER OUTLINE

Thomas O'Donnell's testimony highlights the marginal existence of many working-class Americans in the late nineteenth century. The responses of congressional committee members to his story show that they are far more familiar with the fruits of industrial progress than with its underside.

The Texture of Industrial Progress

    The Rise of Heavy Industry from 1880 to 1900
    Financing Postwar Growth
    Railroads: Pioneers of Big Business
    Growth in Other Industries
    The Erratic Economic Cycle

Urban Expansion in the Industrial Age

    A Growing Population
    American Urban Dwellers
    The New Immigration: 1880-1900
    The Industrial City: 1880-1900
    Neighborhoods and Neighborhood Life
    Streetcar Suburbs
    The Social Geography of the Cities

The Life of the Middle Class

New Freedoms for Middle-Class Women
Male Mobility and the Success Ethic

Industrial Work and the Laboring Class

The Impact of Ethnic Diversity
The Changing Nature of Work
Work Settings and Experiences
The Worker's Share in Industrial Progress
The Family Economy
Women at Work

Capital Versus Labor

On-the-Job Protests
Strike Activity After 1876
Labor Organizing: 1865-1900
The Knights of Labor and the AFL
Working-Class Setbacks
The Homestead and Pullman Strikes of 1892 and 1894
The Balance Sheet

Conclusion: The Complexity of Industrial Capitalism

(2) SIGNIFICANT THEMES AND HIGHLIGHTS

1. This chapter examines America's industrial trans-
    formation between 1865 and 1900 and highlights its
    special characteristics. The importance of big
    business, the rise of heavy industry, rapid
    urbanization, and the growth of an industrial work
    force are described as well as the unpredictable
    nature of the economic cycle and its impact on life.
    The testimony of Thomas O'Donnell reveals how one
    working-class American family fared in this period.

2. The chapter outlines the changing physical and social
    arrangements of the late nineteenth century and the
    varied living and working conditions for its
    various groups. In most cities, people were
    separated by class, ethnicity, and occupation, which
    often led to social distance, ignorance, prejudice,
    and sometimes even violence.

3. The world of work and its mixed blessings and burdens
    are described for working-class and middle-class
    Americans.

4. The various conflicts between capital and labor
    provide the material for the chapter's conclusion.
    Several of the major strikes are analyzed in detail,
    although the chapter emphasizes why most working-
    class Americans did not support unions.

(3) LEARNING GOALS

Familiarity with Basic Knowledge

After reading this chapter, you should be able to:

1. List three ways in which big business contributed to
    economic growth and three reason why big business
    contributed to economic instability.

2. Describe the physical and social arrangements of the
    industrial city and neighborhood life.

3. Describe important changes in middle-class life.

4. Show how late-nineteenth-century industrialism changed
    the composition of the work force and state why
    working-class Americans often had to depend on the labor
    of their children.

5. Point out the different positions taken by workers and
    their bosses on the pace of production, individualism,
    and union activity.

6. Describe two major incidents of working-class activism
    and their outcomes.

Practice in Historical Thinking Skills

After reading this chapter, you should be able to:

1. Discuss the extent and importance of occupational
    mobility for the American working class.

2. Explain why working-class Americans were often
    reluctant to join unions.

3. Discuss the role ethnicity played in working-class life.

(4) ENRICHMENT IDEAS

1. Using the RTP directions as a beginning, seek out material about late-nineteenth-century life by reading selected congressional hearings. What kinds of people are called upon to give testimony? How do congressional committee members respond to their testimony? Do you think there is much sympathy for the situation of working-class Americans?

2. What might a union organizer say to persuade the steelworkers that it was in their best interest to join the union? What might the responses be from each of the various ethnic groups in that community? From the native-born Americans? How might the managers respond?

3. Imagine yourself to be an immigrant from eastern Europe who has come to the United States for work. If you were to write a letter to relatives at home, would you tell them to join you or not? What would some of your comments be about housing, work, and opportunity?

4. Some of your relatives may well have migrated to this country in the early years of this century. Ask your grandparents and parents. This offers an excellent opportunity for an oral history (see RTP for Chapter 26) as well as an investigation of family mementos and photographs.

Instructor:

5. Photographs of urban life by Jacob Riis and others can provide the basis for a slide lecture and in-class analysis of urban conditions as well as for a paper. They offer an excellent opportunity for students to consider the photographer's point of view. (See RTP for Chapter 22.)

6. The Storm of Strangers film series highlights the experience of various immigrants groups and can lead to a discussion of the importance of ethnicity in American life. Hester Street raises questions about the inevitable clash between Americanization and preserving ethnic identity.

7. Have two students role-play a conversation between John D. Rockefeller and one of his workers about the benefits of working for Standard Oil and the

benefits Standard Oil makes to economic growth. Rockefeller's comment that "the day of individual competition . . . is past and gone" can be a starting point for either a lecture or a discussion of consolidation and the results for American life.

8. This chapter can provide the basic information for an urban walking tour and visit to a factory. Even factories built in the twentieth century can give students a sense of what industrial labor was like for nineteenth-century workers. A city atlas like Sanbourn's Atlas can also help students understand new urban patterns and some of their implications for social, economic, and cultural life. This exercise can easily be structured as a paper assignment.

9. Two novels, Theodore Dreiser's Sister Carrie and Stephen Crane's Maggie: A Girl of the Streets, offer good opportunities for analyzing the urban experience and the limited opportunities available for working-class girls. Thomas Bell's Out of This Furnace and Upton Sinclair's The Jungle vividly describe the immigrant experience in factories and cities.

10. The importance of immigration to working-class culture, protest, and apathy can be further explored, especially when accompanied by an exercise in which students have explored their own immigrant, working-class origins. See Chapters 3 and 4 in Nash, Retracing the Past, Volume Two.

(5) FURTHER RESOURCES

Documentaries and Films

1. Alistair Cooke's America. Episodes 8, Money on the Land (55 mins.; the rise of industrial America) and 9, The Huddled Masses (53 mins.)

2. The Chinese Americans: The Early Immigrants (20 mins.; features paintings, photographs, prints as well as live action)

3. Hester Street (a superb full-length film on the Jewish immigrant experience on the Lower East Side of New York and the dilemmas of assimilation)

4. The Turnaround (28 mins.; focuses on the Homestead strike in 1892 and its impact on the union movement)

5. <u>The Age of Uncertainty II: The Manners and Morals of High Capitalism</u> (57 mins.; narrated by John Kenneth Galbraith, film casts a critical and amusing look at the lives of big business leaders in the late nineteenth century)

Slides and Photographs

1. <u>American History Slide Collection,</u> groups L, N, O, and P (excellent photographs of cities, immigrants, industrial workers, factories, railroads, advertisements, and other visual pictures of late-nineteenth-century American life)

2. Otto L. Bettman, <u>The Good Old Days--They Were Terrible!</u> (delightful picture album of late-nineteenth-century American life from the Bettman Archives)

Recordings

1. <u>Railroading Songs: More American Voices</u> (folk songs of America's minorities) and <u>Farm Songs/City Songs,</u> (audiocassettes from Oscar Brand's American Folksong Archive)

2. <u>The Hand That Holds the Bread: Progress and Protest in the Gilded Age: Songs from the Civil War to the Columbian Exposition</u> (New World Records)

20

Politics and Reform

(1) CHAPTER OUTLINE

Edward Bellamy's utopian novel, <u>Looking Backward,</u> contrasts the class divisions and competition of the nineteenth century with a harmonious, cooperative, imaginary future society. The novel captures the fears and concerns of middle-class Americans as they struggled to cope with and reform an age marked by serious inequalities of wealth and political neglect.

Politics in the Gilded Age

Politics, Parties, Patronage, and Presidents
National Issues
The Lure of Local Politics

Middle-Class Reform

The Gospel of Wealth
Reform Darwinism and Pragmatism
Settlements and Social Gospel
Reforming the City
The Struggle for Women's Suffrage

The Pivotal 1890s

Republican Legislation in the Early 1890s
The Depression of 1893
The Crucial Election of 1896
The New Shape of American Politics

Conclusion: Looking Forward

(2) SIGNIFICANT THEMES AND HIGHLIGHTS

1. Bellamy's novel, Looking Backward, revealed the fears
    and concerns of many middle-class Americans as
    urbanization, industrial strife, and immigration
    changed the face of a once familiar America. The chapter
    describes the increasing attention of middle-class
    reformers, many of them Christian intellectuals and
    women social settlement workers, to urban and other ills
    in American society. The most serious concern was the
    growing inequality of wealth, fictionalized in Bellamy's
    coach scene but actualized in the depression of the mid-
    1890s.

2. National politics, marked by high voter turnouts and
    locked in a stalemate between the two major parties,
    ignored the needs of farmers, workers, and other
    ordinary Americans, and did little to remedy
    inequalities of wealth. This chapter draws a sharp
    contrast between the issues faced (and ignored) at the
    national level and the lure of such issues as education,
    temperance, nationality, and race, which were hotly
    contested in local and state politics.

3. Politics and reform are brought together not only in
    cities but also in the Populist revolt and the election
    of 1896, which marked the 1890s as a "pivotal" turning
    point in American attitudes and political party
    alignments.

(3) LEARNING GOALS

Familiarity with Basic Knowledge

After reading this chapter, you should be able to:

1. Characterize Gilded Age politicians, party campaigns,
    and the two political parties; and briefly explain the

three major national and three typical local political issues of the late nineteenth century.

2.   Define the following terms: Gospel of Wealth, social Darwinism, reform Darwinism, pragmatism, Social Gospel, Gilded Age.

3.   Describe the purpose and the programs of the settlement house movement, the Social Gospel, and urban reformers.

4.   State and briefly explain the results of two or three areas of legislation Congress considered in 1890, and explain the causes of the depression of 1893-1897.

5.   Explain the party strategies, campaign issues, and results of the election of 1896.

Practice in Historical Thinking Skills

After reading this chapter, you should be able to:

1.   Analyze the relationship between national and local politics in the Gilded Age and the middle-class movement for reform.

2.   Explain the motivations and programs of urban reformers, the Social Gospel and settlement workers, and those seeking women's suffrage.

3.   Analyze the significance of the election of 1896 as a response to the crises of the pivotal 1890s.

(4) ENRICHMENT IDEAS

1.   Material culture can provide insights in recovering the social and political life of the past. The study of material artifacts generated by the campaign of 1896 reveals much about the values and issues of American political life. But so also can such items as mail-order catalogs, which show dress styles and the goods purchased by Americans in a given age. Compare a recent Sears, Roebuck catalog to one from the Gilded Age. What similarities and differences in middle-class life and consumption patterns are suggested? What do you conclude about leisure and gender roles? What do the buttons, bumper stickers, and material artifacts of a recent political campaign show about contemporary political behavior?

2. To what extent do middle-class men and women play a role in local, state, or national politics today? Identify and interview some persons active in politics. Find out what their concerns are, why they are active, and how effective they think they are. Then compare them to the middle-class reformers of the 1890s.

3. The excitement of the Democratic party convention in 1896 and Bryan's "Cross of Gold" speech is worth special research and attention. So is the election itself. Whose side would you have been on? Why?

Instructor

4. As an extension of the assignments suggested in items 1-3, all of them suitable for written reports and class discussions, students can compare the extent to which middle-class men and women today encounter role confusion and conflicting pressures between their private and public lives with the experiences of men and women in the late nineteenth century.

5. Middle-class magazines can provide the basis for an exploration of middle-class attitudes and values. Ladies Home Journal reveals new ideas about women. Women's fashions reflect and influence changing norms. (See Lois Banner, American Beauty.)

6. A lecture on Jane Addams, or a student assignment based on Twenty Years at Hull House, can reveal the character of the settlement house movement, women's reform role, and its limits.

7. A lecture on family life that expands upon material in this chapter and includes a treatment of adolescence (see Joseph Kett's Rites of Passage: Adolescence in America) should interest students.

8. Bryan's "Cross of Gold" speech provides an excellent opportunity to lecture on or discuss a variety of topics: political party conventions, American political rhetoric, populist and agrarian attitudes, and the changing nature of the Democratic party.

9. The World's Columbian Exposition illustrates the material progress of the period--the world of middle-class America--and serves as an ironic comment on its racist attitudes. See Robert Ridell's "The World's Columbian Exposition of 1893: Racist Underpinnings of a Utopian Artifact," Journal of American Culture 2 (1978).

(5) FURTHER RESOURCES

Documentaries and Films

1. <u>The Age of Uncertainty</u>. Part 2, <u>Manners and Morals of High Capitalism</u> (60 mins.; narrated by John Kenneth Galbraith, highlights the world of big capitalists)

2. <u>American Realists</u>. Part 1, <u>Eighteenth and Nineteenth Centuries</u> (23 mins.; history of painting until 1913)

3. <u>Creative Americans, 1800-1900</u> (28 mins.; shows major cultural achievements)

4. <u>An Invention Called Childhood</u> (40 mins.; traces the development of the notion of childhood)

Recordings

<u>The Hand That Holds the Bread: Progress and Protest in the Gilded Age: Songs from the Civil War to the Columbian Exposition</u> (New World Records)

21

Becoming a World Power

(1) CHAPTER OUTLINE

As the United States Senate debates whether to annex the Philippine Islands, tension mounts near Manila as Filipinos and Americans confront each other across an uneasy neutral zone. While on patrol, Private William Grayson encounters some Filipino soldiers and kills them, and general hostilities break out. The result is a nasty three-year war of suppression, marking a crucial change in America's role in the world.

Steps Toward Empire

America as a Model Society
Early Expansionism
Expansion After Seward

Expansionism in the 1890s

Profits: Searching for Overseas Markets
Patriotism: Asserting National Power
Piety: The Missionary Impulse
Politics: Manipulating Public Opinion

Cuba and the Philippines

The Road to War
"A Splendid Little War"

The Philippines Debates and War
Expansionism Triumphant

Roosevelt's Energetic Diplomacy

Foreign Policy as Darwinian Struggle
Taking the Panama Canal
Policeman of the Caribbean
Opening the Door to China
Japan and the Balance of Power
Preventing War in Europe

Conclusion: The Responsibilities of Power

(2) SIGNIFICANT THEMES AND HIGHLIGHTS

1. The opening anecdote highlights the American annexation of the Philippines by the Senate and the three-year war suppressing the revolt that followed. This episode reflects the major motivations, policies, and problems of American expansionism in the period from 1890 to 1912, the focus of this chapter.

2. The Philippine experience and the wider expressions of expansionism during this period reflect and reveal fundamental and enduring dilemmas of America's relationship with the rest of the world. These ripples start as far back as the Puritans and flow forward to familiar patterns of foreign affairs in our own time.

3. Historical analogies are dangerous, and one must be cautious in making them. Human situations and international relations are never exactly the same. Nevertheless, many are similar enough to be instructive. This chapter can be read, therefore, to understand not only the foreign policy events between 1890 and 1912 but also those in America's recent past and, indeed, those reported in today's newspaper.

4. Although some effort has been made to reflect the common soldier's war experiences, ordinary people play less of a role in this chapter than in others. At the center is an era in foreign affairs in which the United States became a world power. Leading the way was Theodore Roosevelt, a most uncommon person.

Familarity with Basic Knowledge

After reading this chapter, you should be able to:

1. Identify two or three major foreign policy pronouncements that influenced nineteenth-century American policies.

2. Explain each of the four major motivations for American expansionism in the 1890s.

3. Describe the series of events that led to the Spanish-American War and those that led to the annexation of and war with the Philippines.

4. State several arguments for and against the annexation of the Philippines.

5. Locate each of the following on a map and state why it is important.

Cuba	Panama Canal
Guam	Portsmouth, New Hampshire
Hawaiian Islands	Puerto Rico
Hong Kong	Philippine Islands
Manchuria	Samoan Islands
Manila	Santo Domingo (Dominican
Morocco	Republic)
	Venezuela

6. Explain the principles of Theodore Roosevelt's foreign policy and describe the role of the United States in Asia, Europe, and the Caribbean between 1890 and 1912.

Practice in Historical Thinking Skills

After reading this chapter, you should be able to:

1. Compare and contrast American involvement with the Cubans and with the Filipinos, and develop your own position either supporting or rejecting the annexation of the Philippines.

2. Assess the effectiveness of Roosevelt's foreign policy.

3. Evaluate the extent to which the United States continues to experience dilemmas in its international relationships.

(4) ENRICHMENT IDEAS

1. As suggested by the RTP, find other political cartoons about Teddy Roosevelt and American foreign policy during this period (or about other subjects: Bryan, McKinley, and the elections of 1896 and 1900, for example), and analyze how they make their editorial point.

2. On a map of the continental United States, fill in the various parts of the expanding territory of the United States from 1783 to 1853, indicating how each new section was acquired. On a map of the world, locate and fill in all U.S. acquisitions (and interventions) around the world from the Civil War to World War I. What obvious conclusions do you draw?

3. Consider the extent to which the United States still tries to do good in an imperfect world and seeks to be both powerful and loved. Is the United States today basically isolationist or internationalist? To what extent is America still a model for the rest of the world?

4. Historical analogies: The Greek historian Thucydides, writing 2,400 years ago, said that, human nature being what it is, "events which happened in the past . . . will, at some time or other and in much the same ways, be repeated in the future." Despite the wisdom of one of the earliest and greatest historians, historical analogies are dangerous, and one must be cautious in making them. Human situations and international relations, although similar, are never exactly the same.

   Nevertheless, many Americans have drawn an analogy between the war against Aguinaldo's rebels following the annexation of the Philippines and the war in Vietnam in the 1960s and early 1970s. Many have continued the analogy to our relationship with and role in Central America in the 1980s. What do you think of these historical analogies? Is it helpful to make them or not? Is current American foreign policy better or worse served by comparing the Central American situation to Vietnam or to the Philippines? What are the dangers of making historical analogies?

   Consider other historical analogies and the extent to which they inform and enhance understanding or mislead and lead to dangerous decisions. Examples:

Secretary of State Dean Rusk's frequent comparison of a weak policy toward North Vietnam in the mid-1960s with England's appeasement policy toward Nazi Germany in the 1930s; or the argument of people who oppose increased nuclear weapons because earlier arms races in history, like that between Germany and England before World War I, always led to war. What others can you think of?

Instructor:

5. Adapt and use the historical analogies idea for a guaranteed lively discussion, especially following a reading assignment and paper topic exploring the issues.

6. Ask students to develop a reasoned argument and prepare a speech either for or against the annexation of the Philippines. Bring to class, which meets as the U.S. Senate in January 1899. Debate and vote. Then discuss the role-playing exercise, its dynamics, and its results. This can be done in a large lecture class as well as smaller ones, for example, by the not unhistorical act of stretching the Constitution in order to have the matter decided by a joint resolution of the full Congress.

7. Ask students to have a debate on the questions, Were Americans imperialistic in 1898? Are they now? Or use these questions as the dramatic focus for a lecture analyzing the motivations for and manifestations of expansionism as they still apply today.

8. Have students describe one of the events discussed in this chapter from the perspective of the Cubans, Filipinos, or Chinese involved. Then ask students to think about how these groups see us today.

9. Who Invited Us? is a documentary that criticizes American involvement (particularly in Central America) since the Spanish-American War. It can stimulate discussion on American foreign policy as well as encourage an evaluation of the filmmaker's assumptions and point of view.

10. Documents such as the Roosevelt Corollary, his Naval College speech in 1897, the full text of McKinley's prayer about the Philippines, Hay's Open Door notes, and the poems, speeches, and essays by anti-imperialists can be handed out and discussed in class or shown on an overhead projector and analyzed by the instructor.

(5) FURTHER RESOURCES

Photographs

A Cartoon History of the Spanish American War (16 reproductions), and Teddy Roosevelt: A Cartoon History (21 reproductions), available from Documentary Photo Aids

PART FIVE

A MODERNIZING PEOPLE
1900−1945

22

The Progressives Confront Industrial Capitalism

(1) CHAPTER OUTLINE

A young midwestern lawyer, Frances Kellor, trains herself as a social reformer because she believes in the progressive faith that moral vision and efficient expertise can eliminate poverty and inequality. As the first woman appointed to head a state agency, she is one of the leaders of the effort to foster both social justice and middle-class values for immigrant workers in America.

The Social Justice Movement

The Progressive World View
The Muckrakers
Working Women and Children
Home and School
Crusades Against Saloons, Brothels, and
Movie Houses

The Worker in the Progressive Era

Adjusting to Industrial Labor
Union Organizing
Garment Workers and the Triangle Fire
Radical Labor

Reform in the Cities and States

> Municipal Reformers
> The City Beautiful
> Reform in the States

Theodore Roosevelt and the Square Deal

> A Strong and Controversial President
> Dealing with the Trusts
> Meat Inspection and Pure Food and Drugs
> Conservation
> Progressivism for Whites Only
> William Howard Taft
> The Election of 1912

Woodrow Wilson and the New Freedom

> Tariff and Banking Reform
> Moving Closer to a New Nationalism

Conclusion: The Limits of Progressivism

(2) SIGNIFICANT THEMES AND HIGHLIGHTS

1. The work of Frances Kellor reflects the twin goals of urban professional reformers in their response to industrialism, immigration, and urbanism. They sought to achieve social justice and reform as well as order and efficiency. Their faith in social research and expert commissions to solve social problems was nearly as strong as their optimism that they would succeed in cleaning up America.

2. Kellor's life also reveals the progressives' ambiguous attitude toward the poor immigrant workers they sought to help. Progressive reformers were well-intentioned and sincere in their desire to alleviate social misery and expand opportunity at the same time as they were paternalistic, elitist, and racist in their effort to make immigrants into good Americanized citizens with middle-class values.

3. In this chapter, the work of progressive reformers is shown at the three political levels of American society--cities, states, and the national government, where the differences between the New Nationalism of Theodore Roosevelt and the New Freedom of Woodrow Wilson are described.

4. Throughout the chapter, note the important role of women in progressive reform and the underlying tone of moral concern and family values that permeated the movement.

(3) LEARNING GOALS

Familiarity with Basic Knowledge

After reading this chapter, you should be able to:

1. Enumerate and briefly describe several reform goals of the progressives and their views on child labor, working women, education, and vice.

2. Outline the differing goals and programs for factory reform held by working-class leaders and by progressives.

3. List and briefly describe the major goals and programs of municipal reformers and progressive reformers at the state level.

4. Describe Theodore Roosevelt's attitudes toward and programs for trusts, conservation, and blacks and show how they differed from those of William Howard Taft.

5. Describe the Progressive party and its programs.

6. State the major pieces of progressive legislation passed during the presidency of Woodrow Wilson.

Practice in Historical Thinking Skills

After reading this chapter, you should be able to:

1. Explain the tension among progressives between their twin goals of achieving social justice reform on the one hand and order and efficiency on the other.

2. Compare and contrast the political philosophy of Roosevelt's New Nationalism and Wilson's New Freedom.

3. Assess the success of the progressive movement by analyzing its achievements and limitations.

(4) ENRICHMENT IDEAS

1. Using the examples in the textbook or a larger collection of photographs of urban slums, street children, and immigrant workers by Jacob Riis and Lewis Hine, analyze the photographs and discuss the questions in the RTP dealing with the use of the documentary photograph for purposes of reform.

2. Make a chart showing the similarities and differences between the political ideals, policies, and programs of Theodore Roosevelt and those of Woodrow Wilson.

Instructor:

3. Send students out with their cameras to take pictures of contemporary issues of social concern, and arrange the developed photographs into a show. Discuss the point of view and purposes of the photographers and the extent to which they heighten or distort reality. From this exercise in contemporary uses of the camera, return to the early part of the century and evaluate the effectiveness of progressive photographic reformers.

4. Have students imagine themselves as a blue-ribbon study commission of typical young progressive experts meeting to discuss the ills of American society in, say, 1910. Ask them to put together a list of concerns and decide upon a specific program of recommendations. Half the group, however, should be instructed to be primarily interested in relieving the social misery of suffering Americans by providing social justice and equal opportunity, while the other half is told to be primarily interested in order, efficiency, and making these Americans into good citizens with middle-class values. This is an exercise not only in identifying the main progressive issues but also in experiencing the tension and ambiguity in the progressive approach to reform. A large lecture class could be divided in half to represent these two sides of progressivism as a dramatic way of underlining the ambiguity during your lecture on the subject. See Chapters 10-12 in Nash, Retracing the Past, Volume Two.

5. To see how much of that tension still exists, ask students to repeat the exercise in item 4, but for 1990 instead of 1910.

6. Build a lecture or discussion around viewing any of the films noted in section 5. An especially effective class can be based on the cassette-slide presentation of "The Distorted Image: Stereotype and Caricature in American Popular Graphics, 1850-1922," available from the Anti-Defamation League of B'Nai B'Rith.

7. Students can be invited to consider the case of a young single woman, perhaps someone like Carrie in Theodore Drieser's novel <u>Sister Carrie</u> (1900), who leaves the safety of her midwestern farm family for the adventurous glitter and manifold opportunities of life in Chicago. She finds, however, that working and living in Chicago is not nearly as exciting and rewarding as she had thought, and she faces a crisis of choice over becoming a prostitute or a mistress, struggling on in her factory job under terrible conditions, or returning home. Discussion can focus on the several options she faces, the pros and cons of each one, and what option students think she will choose. This exercise can be done either in small groups, in which differences of opinion should enliven discussion, or as individual writing assignments.

8. Re-create the campaign and election of 1912 by dividing the class into four groups representing each of the four parties. Depending on the time you wish to devote to this exercise, you can have students write and present party platforms, give campaign speeches, debate issues, and eventually hold a mock election.

9. A lecture on the development of socialism in the United States would supplement the material in the chapter effectively and could be linked to the discussion in Chapter 19 of the limited appeal of unionism. Moreover, you can raise important questions about historical interpretations by presenting Gabriel Kolko's analysis of progressivism, found in <u>The Triumph of Conservatism.</u>

(5) FURTHER RESOURCES

Documentaries and Films

1. <u>A Storm of Strangers: Jewish America</u> (27 mins.), <u>Chinese America</u> (26 mins.), <u>The Irish</u> (30 mins.), <u>Italian American</u> (26 mins.; each shows the way in which the group dealt with new conditions in the United States)

2. Cry of Children (28 mins.; made in 1912, reveals reform mentality)

3. Northern Lights (95 mins.; award-winning film focusing on a little-known agrarian movement on the Great Plains among first- and second-generation Scandinavians)

4. Junction City, 1890-1915 (27 mins.; using documentary photographs, film shows the development of a small Kansas town into a city and some of the human consequences of growth)

5. Before the Nickelodeon (60 mins.; traces filmmaking from 1896 to 1909 and the shifting ideas of the medium, from newspaper to film as entertainment)

6. Women's Rights in the U.S.: An Informal History (27 mins.; a dialogue between feminists and antifeminists)

7. Focus on 1900-1909 (58 mins; portrayal of the decade, using rare documentary footage)

8. America & Lewis Hine (56 mins; an award-winning, critically acclaimed documentary that portrays the development of industrial America during the first four decades of the twentieth century)

9. The Shadow Catchers: Edward S. Curtis and the North American Indian (88 mins.; brilliant study of an anthropologist filmmaker's work with Native Americans, including rare footage of Northwest coast Indians)

Slides and Photographs

1. The American History Slide Collection

2. The Distorted Image: Stereotype and Caricature in American Popular Graphics, 1850-1922 (60 slides with cassette tapes based on the work of John J. Appel and Selma Appel), available from the Anti-Defamation League of B'Nai B'Rith

3. The Feminist Revolution (26 photos), Immigration (40 photos), and Child Labor (15 photographs), available from Documentary Photo Aids

23

The Great War

(1) CHAPTER OUTLINE

Edmund Arpin joins the army in 1917 less out of patriotism than out of a desire for excitement. In the Great War, he discovers that modern conflict is neither heroic nor noble. Nevertheless, his wartime adventures and the sense of common purpose he gains through his participation in the war effort make World War I a critical event in his life.

The Early Years of the War

    The Causes of War
    American Reactions
    The New Military Technology
    Difficulties of Neutrality
    World Trade and Neutrality Rights
    Intervening in Mexico and Central America

The United States Enters the War

    The Election of 1916
    Deciding for War
    A Patriotic Crusade
    Raising an Army

The Military Experience

    The American Doughboy

The Black Soldier
Over There

Domestic Impact of the War

Financing the War
Increasing Federal Power
War Workers
The Climax of Progressivism
Suffrage for Women

Planning for Peace

The Paris Peace Conference
Women for Peace
Wilson's Failed Dream

Conclusion: The Divided Legacy of the Great War

(2) SIGNIFICANT THEMES AND HIGHLIGHTS

1. As the anecdote about Edmund Arpin suggests, World
    War I affected the lives of Americans in many ways.
    Black and white soldiers helped make important
    contributions to victory. War brought new taxes and
    jobs, increased the power of the central government,
    and, as always, resulted in inflation.

2. The chapter explores American foreign policy before,
    during, and after the Great War. In these years,
    Wilson betrayed some of his democratic ideals and
    showed the basic continuity of American foreign
    policy by frequent interventions in Central America.
    When war broke out in Europe, Wilson's attempt to
    keep the country neutral were undermined by basic
    American sympathy for the Allies, economic ties with
    Great Britain and France, and U-boat incidents on the
    seas. Once at war, Wilson harbored dreams of a just
    peace. Although realizing some of his goals at the
    Versailles Peace Conference, Wilson was forced to
    make major concessions to the Allies, who did not
    share his idealistic vision of the world. He also
    lost the battle at home when the Senate refused to
    ratify the treaty.

3. The need for support in the election of 1916 prodded
    Wilson to promote various social reform measures
    advocated by progressives. Ironically, although
    reformers feared war, the war years represented the

climax of the progressive movement. Once war was declared, the government carried on a gigantic propaganda campaign to persuade Americans of the war's noble purpose. These overzealous patriotic efforts led to violations of civil rights and antiforeign crusades at home.

(3) LEARNING GOALS

Familarity with Basic Knowledge

After reading this chapter, you should be able to:

1. List four things that made American neutrality almost impossible.

2. Show how Wilson's policy toward central America was an extension of both "big-stick" diplomacy and dollar diplomacy.

3. Explain why the Russian Revolution seemed to jeopardize Wilson's hopes for the postwar world.

4. Show the connections between the work of the Creel committee and antiforeign and antiradical activities.

5. Compare the military experience of the United States with those of Great Britain and France.

Practice in Historical Thinking Skills

After reading this chapter, you should be able to:

1. Analyze how the war was, in an ironic sense, the climax of progressivism.

2. Assess Wilson's successes at the Versailles Peace Conference and his failures at home.

3. Analyze Wilson as a reluctant social reformer.

(4) ENRICHMENT IDEAS

1. You may have relatives who were alive during World War I. Whether they were in the army or at home, you have a good opportunity to do some interviewing. Were their experiences in any way similar to those described in this chapter? Do they remember any government propaganda films? Did the war change their lives in any significant way? What do they remember most vividly about the war and why?

2. There are many good novels about World War I to read. Some of the best known are Ernest Hemingway's <u>Farewell to Arms</u>, Erich Remarque's <u>All Quiet on the Western Front</u>, and John Dos Passos's <u>1919</u>.

3. You could investigate newspaper accounts of events like the sinking of the <u>Lusitania</u> to ascertain how "neutral" the American press was. Also check the editorial pages for articles and cartoons that suggest American sympathies. Magazines are also a good source for attitudes toward the war and may show the attempts to stir up patriotism.

Instructor:

4. A hot discussion item is to ask students whether they think war promotes or retards social reform. An examination of World War I songs, recruiting posters, cartoons, editorials, anti-VD films (as in the RTP), and other forms of propaganda can serve to initiate a discussion about the war experience both at home and abroad. These can also be used in a lecture format. See Chapter 13 in Nash, <u>Retracing the Past</u>, Volume Two.

5. A class devoted to race relations during the war can be based on work by William Tuttle (<u>Race Riot: Chicago in the Red Summer of 1919</u>), Elliott Rudwick (<u>Race Riot at East St. Louis</u>), Robert Haynes (<u>A Night of Violence</u>), and David Kennedy (<u>Over Here</u>).

6. Have students prepare papers developing an argument for or against the Senate ratification of the Treaty of Versailles and membership in the League of Nations. Once they have developed their positions, they can carry on a live debate, take a vote, and then analyze the results and what they learned from the experience.

7. Students can study each of Wilson's Fourteen
    Points, evaluate the impact they might have on the
    world order, and then critique them from Lenin's
    point of view. This exercise highlights the tensions
    between two conflicting visions of world order. You
    could also use this basic idea as the framework for a
    lecture.

8. Using various psychobiographies of Woodrow Wilson
    (Freud and Bullitt, for example) and James Barber's
    The Presidential Character: Predicting Performance in
    the White House as sources, you can lecture on Wilson
    at the same time as introducing students to the
    possibilities and pitfalls of applying psychological
    and other social science theories to historical
    figures.

(5) FURTHER RESOURCES

Documentaries and Films

1. Goodbye Billy: America Goes to War, 1917-1918 (25
    mins.; features old songs and film clips to show
    emotional response to conflict)

2. The Great War (54 mins.; shows events leading up to
    and consequences of war)

3. Mirror of America (36 mins.; film from the Ford
    Historical Film Collection at the National Archives;
    shows famous and ordinary people between 1915 and
    1920)

4. The Ordeal of Woodrow Wilson (26 mins.; focuses on
    failure to win approval of Versailles Treaty)

5. Focus on 1910-19 (58 mins; overview of the decade
    with documentary footage)

Slides and Photographs

1. American History Slide Collection

2. Pro and Anti War Cartoons of World War I (20
    reproductions) and A Cartoon History of U.S.
    Involvement in World War I (16 reproductions)
    available from Documentary Photo Aids (see the RTP
    for Chapter 21)

24

Affluence and Anxiety

(1) CHAPTER OUTLINE

Two black Alabama sharecroppers, John and Lizzie Parker, move north during World War I in search of jobs, opportunity, a home of their own, and an education for their children. Eventually they reach Detroit, with its promise of wartime jobs in the automotive industry. As the decade of the 1920s develops, the Parkers experience racial hatred; uncertain, part-time work; a half-finished house on an unpaved ghetto street; and a completed high school degree for their daughter Sally.

Postwar Problems

>   Red Scare
>   Working-Class Protest
>   Ku Klux Klan
>   The Sacco-Vanzetti Case

A Prospering Economy

>   The Rising Standard of Living
>   The Rise of the Modern Corporation
>   Electrification
>   Automobile Culture
>   The Exploding Metropolis
>   A Communications Revolution

Hopes Raised, Promises Deferred

Clash of Values
Immigration and Migration
Marcus Garvey: Black Messiah
The Harlem Renaissance and the Lost Generation
Women Struggle for Equality
Rural America in the 1920s
The Workers' Share of Prosperity

The Business of Politics

Harding and Coolidge
Herbert Hoover
Foreign Policy in the 1920s
The Survival of Progressivism
Temperance Triumphant
The Election of 1928
Stock Market Crash

Conclusion: A New Era of Prosperity and Problems

(2) SIGNIFICANT THEMES AND HIGHLIGHTS

1. The dominant theme of the decade of the 1920s, as the Parkers' story suggests, was the mixed fulfillment of various dreams of suburban comfort and success. In a decade in which general prosperity, quick riches in the stock market, and new technologies held out the promise of success to all, many, like John and Lizzie Parker, found their dream always just out of reach.

2. The 1920s, neatly packed between the end of World War I and the stock market crash in 1929, was a decade of paradox and contradiction. Conflicting trends persisted throughout the decade: prosperity and poverty, optimism and disillusionment, inventiveness and intolerance, flamboyant heroism and fallen idols, anxiety and affluence. Many Americans, like the Parkers and the New Era decade itself, saw their hopes raised and then deferred or dashed.

3. This chapter illustrates the profound effects that technological developments (the automobile, radio, the bathroom, for example) have on diverse aspects of people's lives.

4. Interwoven throughout the chapter are the hopes and fears of many different groups--blacks in northern cities, migrant Mexicans and other immigrants, nativist Americans in the Ku Klux Klan and other patriotic organizations, women, white suburbanites, factory workers, sports and media heroes, disillusioned writers, temperance crusaders, optimistic investors and advertisers, and many others.

(3) LEARNING GOALS

Familiarity with Basic Knowledge

After reading this chapter, you should be able to:

1. Describe the postwar mood in America and the strikes, race riots, and Palmer raids of 1919 and 1920.

2. Name several technological inventions and influential ideas of the New Era and their impact on social and economic life.

3. Outline the development, distribution, and discrepancies of prosperity in the 1920s.

4. Describe the presidential style and administrations of Harding and Coolidge.

5. Outline the foreign policy currents of the United States during the 1920s.

6. Describe the election of 1928 and the stock market crash.

Practice in Historical Thinking Skills

After reading this chapter, you should be able to:

1. Analyze and evaluate the distribution of the benefits of prosperity during the New Era.

2. Analyze the impact of the automobile and other technological developments on American social and economic life in the 1920s.

3. Explain the major paradoxes and contradictions of the 1920s.

(4) ENRICHMENT IDEAS

1. Examine the advertisements in the RTP section to see how they reflect the currents of American culture in the 1920s. What do they suggest about attitudes toward blacks, women, and other groups? What do they reveal about American values and priorities? Now look at any contemporary magazine, watch television, and observe current advertisements. What do you learn about today's attitudes, values, and priorities? What has changed? What has not?

2. It would be quite easy to read some newspapers from the 1920s, either the New York _Times_ or a local newspaper (both of which your library probably has on microfilm). You might focus on the coverage of the Teapot Dome scandal, the Scopes trial, Lindbergh's flight, or the election of 1928. Or you might look at advertising, editorials, and various feature articles to capture the mood of the 1920s.

3. One way to experience the currents of social life during the 1920s is through reading the literature of the time. Such novels as F. Scott Fitzgerald's _The Great Gatsby_ and _Tender Is the Night_; Ernest Hemingway's _The Sun Also Rises_; Sherwood Anderson's _Winesburg, Ohio_; Sinclair Lewis's _Main Street_, _Babbitt_, and _Elmer Gantry_; Claude McKay's _Home to Harlem_; Jean Toomer's _Cane_; John Dos Passos's _1919_ and _The Big Money_; William Faulkner's _The Sound and the Fury_; Theodore Dreiser's _An American Tragedy_; and many others provide wonderful insights into manners and morals. Select one of these, or another novel written in and about the 1920s, read it, and write an essay about how well it reflects the times.

Instructor:

4. The 1920s have been described as the "Jazz Age," or the "roaring twenties." After a lecture on "the other side of the 1920s," students can discuss the extent to which they think these are accurate summary capsules of the decade. Useful sources on both sides include Frederick Lewis Allen, _Only Yesterday,_ and Milton Plesur, ed., _The 1920s: Problems and Paradoxes_.

5. Base a lecture or discussion on the major heroes of the 1920s and what made them heroes. What does who a nation selects as its heroes reveal about national values? Who are our heroes today?

6. Many of the novels mentioned in item 3 have been made into feature films of varying quality and would enhance the course if shown on campus.

7. Considering the high hopes suffragists had, it seems appropriate to consider what happened to the women's movement in the 1920s. Consult William Chafe's The American Woman. Another interesting topic deals with the impact of technology on women's housework and why new machines did not reduce the hours spent on housework. Consult Ruth Cowan's More Work for Mother.

(5) FURTHER RESOURCES

Documentaries and Films

1. Golden Twenties (68 mins.; newsreels showing many sides of the 1920s)

2. Movies Learn to Talk (28 mins.; development of sound movies with excerpts from both silent and talking movies)

3. Alistair Cooke's America. Episode 10, The Promise Fulfilled and the Promise Broken (55 mins.; the 1920s and the 1930s)

4. Focus on the Twenties (58 mins; documentaries illuminate the shift from rural to urban and the character of the decade)

5. The Flapper Story (29 mins.; a lively blend of contemporary interviews and archival film footage examining the social phenomenon of the flapper, the provocative "New Woman" of America's Roaring Twenties)

Filmstrips

What This Country Needs Is a Good Five-Cent Cigar, My Friends Are Keeping Me Awake Nights, and Everyone Ought to Be Rich, available from the American Heritage Media Collection

Photographs

Prohibition: A Cartoon History (14 reproductions) available from Documentary Photo Aids

25

The Great Depression and the New Deal

(1) CHAPTER OUTLINE

The Depression changed Diana Morgan's life, as it did the lives of countless other Americans. It disrupted her comfortable existence and forced her to search for work in order to help her family. Diana's job in a New Deal agency introduced her to the far more serious problems of other Americans and persuaded her of the importance of New Deal efforts in alleviating misery and want.

The Great Depression

The Depression Begins
Hoover and the Depression
The Collapsing Economy
The Bonus Army

Roosevelt and the First New Deal

One Hundred Days
Relief Measures
Agricultural Adjustment Act
Industrial Recovery
Civilian Conservation Corps
Tennessee Valley Authority
Critics of the New Deal

The Second New Deal

> Work Relief and Social Security
> Aiding the Farmers
> Controlling Corporate Power and Taxing the Wealthy
> The New Deal for Labor
> America's Minorities in the 1930s
> Women and the New Deal

The Last Years of the New Deal

> The Election of 1936
> The Battle of the Supreme Court
> The Third New Deal

The Other Side of the 1930s

> Taking to the Road
> The Electric Home
> The Age of Leisure
> Literary Reflections of the 1930s
> Radio's Finest Hour
> The Silver Screen

Conclusion: The Ambivalence of the Great Depression

(2) SIGNIFICANT THEMES AND HIGHLIGHTS

1. As the anecdote about Diana Morgan suggests, the Depression decade was a harsh one for many Americans. Although Hoover moved forcefully to meet the crisis, he failed to stop the economic decline or to gain the confidence of the American people.

2. Although Franklin Roosevelt built on Hoover's beginning, unlike Hoover, he was able to persuade Americans that his programs could solve the country's economic woes. Some characterized his programs as radical, but Roosevelt steered a moderate course with both his recovery measures and his efforts at social justice and reform. He never succeeded, however, in bringing the country out of the Depression.

3. The chapter shows the more positive side of the Depression era. Middle-class Americans were caught up in a communications revolution, enjoyed spectator sports, were fascinated by gadgets, and were interested in travel. The 1930s was a decade defined by the modern kitchen and Walt Disney just as much as

by bread lines and alphabet-soup agencies. This
bright side of the 1930s suggests how hard it is to
generalize about a complex period like the
Depression.

(3) LEARNING GOALS

Familiarity with Basic Knowledge

After reading this chapter, you should be able to:

1. Give three reasons for the deepening economic
    depression and three measures Hoover took to stem the
    Depression.

2. Characterize the first New Deal from 1933 to 1935 and
    name several measures of relief, recovery, and reform
    passed in the first 100 days.

3. Show how the Social Security Act and the Works
    Progress Administration exemplified the move of the
    second New Deal toward goals of social reform and
    social justice.

4. Explain the significance of the Wagner Act and its
    impact on organized labor.

5. Characterize the New Deal's programs for minority
    groups.

6. Give three or four examples of the "other side" of
    the 1930s.

Practice in Historical Thinking Skills

After reading this chapter, you should be able to:

1. Compare and contrast Hoover's and Roosevelt's
    approaches to the Depression.

2. Evaluate the New Deal as the realization of
    progressive dreams.

3. Develop an argument supporting or rejecting the
    chapter author's assessment of the New Deal: "It
    promoted social justice and social reform, but it
    provided very little for those at the bottom of
    American society."

(4) ENRICHMENT IDEAS

1. Enjoy some 1930s movies as historical documents. What do they tell you about the myths, values, and spirit of that decade?

2. Your community may well have a mural painted by the WPA or a park constructed by the CCC. Locate and visit the site to see the kinds of work the government subsidized. What contributions to your community were made by these programs? Similarly, your library probably has a state guide written by WPA teams. Find it and see what kinds of historical and cultural sites were described.

3. In addition to Studs Terkel's <u>Hard Times</u>, a superb oral history of the 1930s, your library may have interesting local collections of primary documents that capture personal responses to the Depression years. You can use them in the same way as you might use the material collected from interviewing family and friends.

4. For a picture of the life of migrant workers in the 1930s, you could read the novel mentioned in the text, John Steinbeck's <u>Grapes of Wrath</u>. For the Depression experience of blacks in the South, see Zora Neale Hurston's <u>Their Eyes Are Watching God,</u> and for black migrants in northern cities, read Richard Wright's <u>Native Son</u>.

Instructor:

5. There are several excellent films that can provide the basis for a discussion of events during the 1930s. <u>Just Around the Corner</u> (53 mins.) gives an overview of the decade and captures several of the personalities mentioned in this chapter. The film points out that New Deal programs never dealt adequately with the country's economic problems. <u>With Babies and Banners</u> (45 mins.) focuses on the Flint sit-down strike and highlights the role of the community's women during the strike. <u>Union Maids</u> (48 mins.) shows the struggles of women labor organizers with male union leaders as well as with corporations. <u>The River</u> (30 mins.) shows the effects of the TVA on erosion, flooding, and poverty in the Mississippi River basin. <u>Herbert Hoover</u> (26 mins.) provides a sympathetic view of Hoover but also gives a good sense of why he failed to capture the confidence of the American people.

6. The film <u>Hollywood Dream Factory</u> (52 mins.) can
    lend itself to a discussion of the other side of
    the 1930s and lead into a discussion or lecture on
    the persistence of traditional American beliefs in
    upward mobility, individualism, and progress even
    during a time of depression. Consult Andrew Bergman,
    <u>We're in the Money: Depression America and Its Films.</u>

7. Divide the class into small groups. Each group will
    consider the question of the New Deal's impact on one
    group of Americans--white women, black sharecroppers,
    businessmen, farmers, workers, and so on. When the
    groups report, there should be a lively discussion of
    New Deal programs and the difficulty of generalizing
    about their impact. Or students could be asked to
    write an editorial on a particular New Deal program
    from the perspective of one of these groups.

8. A lecture devoted to the question, How much did the
    New Deal change the distribution of wealth and power?
    should prove useful.   It might also be interesting
    to consider the New Deal as representing change and
    continuities in American life. Finally, it is
    valuable for students to consider the American
    experience and response to the Depression in light
    of experiences and responses elsewhere in the world.
    Such a comparison can highlight common and unique
    aspects of the New Deal decade. See Chapters 16 and
    17 in Nash, <u>Retracing the Past</u>, Volume Two.

9. Visual materials for slide lectures include magazines
    like <u>Life</u> and <u>Look</u> and Farm Security Administration
    photographs on rural poverty by Dorothea Lange.
    These two different kinds of sources illuminate
    different aspects of the decade.

10. Students can be given excerpts of Roosevelt's first
    inaugural speech or a copy of the entire speech.
    They can analyze the kind of language used and
    Roosevelt's explanation for the country's economic
    difficulties, or they can assess the probable
    psychological impact of the speech. In a similar
    fashion, they can hear recordings of one of
    Roosevelt's fireside chats.

11. The class can debate the statement, "Roosevelt was
    actually capitalism's best friend," or the author's
    claim that the New Deal was harder on men than on
    women. Joseph Lash's book (or the TV series), <u>Eleanor
    and Franklin</u>, will stimulate discussions both of
    Eleanor Roosevelt's contributions to the New Deal

decade and of the relationship between these two strong-willed personalities.

(5) FURTHER RESOURCES

Documentaries and Films

1. Bank Holiday Crisis of 1933 (27 mins.; includes inaugural and a fireside chat)

2. The Election of 1932 (20 mins.; newsreels trace election)

3. Demagogues and Do-Gooders: Noisy Voices of the Depression (18 mins.)

4. Bonus March 1932 (12 mins.; made in 1932)

5. Focus on the '30s (58 mins.; made in 1981, film illuminates highlights of the decade)

6. First Lady of the World: Eleanor Roosevelt (25 mins.; uses stills and films to highlight Eleanor Roosevelt's important role)

7. Life Goes to the Movies. Part 1, The Golden Age of Hollywood (35 mins.; excerpts from the decade's films)

8. Available from the National Audio-Visual Center are the following New Deal government films: The Fight for Life (70 mins.; treats the need for prenatal and obstetrical care), Power and the Land (39 mins.; rural life before and after electrification), and The Land (44 mins.; poverty on the land)

9. The Women of Summer: An Unknown Chapter of American Social History (55 mins.; an NEH documentary on the experimentally successful Bryn Mawr Summer School for women workers, 1921-1938)

10. See also the films listed in Enrichment Idea 5.

Photographs

The Dust Bowl (20 photos) and The Great Depression (32 photos), available from Documentary Photo Aids

26
World War II

(1) CHAPTER OUTLINE

N. Scott Momaday, a Kiowa Indian, grows up during World War II playing games, listening to the radio, and going to movies and football games. The presence of war colors his childhood, however. The games he and his friends play are war games, his parents are both employed because of the war, and he is dismayed when others often mistake him for the Japanese enemy.

The Twisting Road to War

> Foreign Policy in the 1930s
> Neutrality in Europe
> Ethiopia and Spain
> War in Europe
> The Election of 1940
> Lend-Lease
> The Path to Pearl Harbor

The Home Front During the War

> Mobilizing for War
> Patriotic Fervor
> Internment of Japanese-Americans
> Black and Hispanic Americans at War

Social Impact of the War

    Wartime Opportunities
    Women Workers for Victory
    Entertaining the People
    The GIs' War
    Women in Uniform

A War of Diplomats and Generals

    War Aims
    1942: Year of Disaster
    A Strategy for Ending the War
    The Invasion of Europe
    The Politics of Victory
    The Big Three at Yalta
    The Atomic Age Begins

Conclusion: Peace, Prosperity, and International Responsibilities

(2) SIGNIFICANT THEMES AND HIGHLIGHTS

1. Although the United States tried to stand apart from the international crises of the 1930s, some of its policies actually assisted Franco and Mussolini. As war broke out in Europe, the United States hesitantly, but predictably, began to assist Great Britain. It was the Japanese attack at Pearl Harbor, however, that made the American involvement in war official.

2. The American economy finally emerged from its years of depression to produce the equipment and supplies that won the war. The war touched people's lives by uprooting them from their homes, by providing them with jobs, by heightening their sense of patriotism, by both attacking and adding to racial discrimination, and by affecting family patterns. Even the ways in which Americans spent their leisure time bore the imprint of war, as Scott Momaday's childhood games suggest.

3. The United States never formulated specific war goals beyond the obvious one of defeating the enemy as rapidly as possible. The alliance that was necessary for victory was quickly strained by the delay in opening a second front in Europe. In 1945, with victory within reach, serious disagreements about the

future of the world began to surface. The explosion
of the world's first atomic bomb added a new and
frightening element to world diplomacy.

(3) LEARNING GOALS

Familiarity with Basic Knowledge

After reading this chapter, you should be able to:

1. Describe the response of the United States to the
   Ethiopian crisis, the Spanish Civil War, and Japanese
   aggression in China.

2. Show how wartime government agencies and boards
   helped to turn America's economy to wartime goals.

3. Explain the reasons for the internment of Japanese-
   Americans and contrast that policy with that toward
   Italian-Americans and German-Americans.

4. Assess the economic impact of the war on black and
   Hispanic Americans and women.

5. Describe the political and diplomatic concerns that
   became important at the war's end, especially the
   controversy over opening a second front, and explain
   the agreements the United States and the Soviet
   Union reached at Yalta.

Practice in Historical Thinking Skills

After reading this chapter, you should be able to:

1. Explain why the United States used the atomic bomb
   and evaluate the decision militarily, diplomatically,
   and morally.

2. Compare the efforts to whip up patriotic feeling in
   World War II with similar efforts in World War I and
   assess the effectiveness and consequences in each
   case.

3. Discuss racism and attitudes toward women as a part
   of the American wartime experience.

(4) ENRICHMENT IDEAS

1. As the RTP for this chapter shows, World War II offers you the chance to interview family and friends about their wartime experiences. Remember to ask about the home front as well as the experiences of those who went overseas and were engaged in battles. In addition to the many detailed questions suggested in the RTP, essentially you are asking people to respond to the following basic questions: How were you affected by the war? What is your most vivid memory? In what ways did the war affect your generation? How do you think your generation differs from the present one?

2. Family photograph albums are also sources of information about your family's past during the war. Find some photographs to show how people lived during wartime and how the war affected family relationships.

3. Some of the films mentioned in this chapter can be seen on late-night television. How would you characterize them? Do they seem to provide an escape from the realities of war? Do they romanticize war or promote patriotism?

4. Popular music and magazines like Life and Time can also provide clues to the mood of the 1940s. How did the war affect song lyrics and the news magazines? What appeals were made to women listeners and readers? To children? To the old?

Instructor:

5. Base a writing project on an oral history assignment. One way to structure this project is to have students write their own responses to questions about the nature of the war both at home and abroad before they find out what their relatives' experiences were. Students can be asked to explain any differences between their responses and those of their relatives. The paper can focus on the differences and similarities between the two and the reasons for them.

6. The film Rosie the Riveter leads to a lively discussion of the participation of women in the war effort and the subsequent efforts to encourage them to leave factory work for the domesticity of the

149

home. A lecture on the topic can be drawn from William Chafe's <u>The American Woman</u> and from Karen Anderson's <u>Wartime Women: Sex Roles, Family Relations, and the Status of Women During World War II.</u>

7. Wartime propaganda posters issued by government agencies (see American History Slide Collection, group O) make excellent visuals with which to illustrate a lecture on the home front.

8. A debate on the topic "Roosevelt was Hitler's silent partner during the 1930s" can encourage assessment of American policy during that decade. Another hot topic for discussion is a comparison of American racism to that of Hitler's Germany, introduced by a brief lecture.

9. A role play can be set up focusing on the meeting of Roosevelt, Churchill, and Stalin in Teheran in 1943 or Yalta in 1945. Students will need some specific information about their country's experiences in the war, as outlined in a lecture. The role play should cover the topics actually discussed at the meeting: the opening of the second front, the invasion of Japan, and the fate of eastern Europe.

10. Another topic that involves students in small groups, perhaps with role playing, can focus on the decision to use the atomic bomb. Students can be asked to develop a position from the point of view of the military, the navy, scientists working on the Manhattan Project, and Japanese citizens. Or a lecture can be given highlighting the controversial historical interpretations of that event.

11. Roosevelt's Quarantine speech and the Four Freedoms speech can be reproduced for students or shown on an overhead projector to analyze as examples of FDR's thinking about the world crisis at two different points.

(5) FURTHER RESOURCES

Documentaries and Films

1. <u>World War II: Total War</u> (27 mins.)

2. <u>Between the Wars</u>. Part 7, <u>FDR and Hitler: The Dynamics of Power</u> (26 mins.; a thought-provoking contrast)

3.   <u>Between the Wars</u>. Part 8, <u>America in the Pacific</u>: <u>The Clash of Two Cultures</u> (26 mins.)

4.   <u>Guilty by Reason of Race</u> (52 mins.; treats the plight of Japanese-Americans)

5.   <u>Adolf Hitler</u>. Part 1, <u>The Rise to Power</u>, and Part 2, <u>The Fall of the Third Reich</u> (27 mins. each)

6.   <u>Hiroshima-Nagasaki</u> (15 mins.; Japanese film records of the destruction)

7.   <u>The Truman Years: Truman and the Atomic Bomb</u> (15 mins.; the president explains reasons for the bomb's use)

8.   <u>The Decision to Drop the Bomb</u> (35 mins.; report by Chet Huntley includes interviews with those involved)

9.   Government documentaries include <u>World at War</u> (44 mins.; highlights events from 1931 to 1941) and the <u>Why We Fight</u> series (shown to Americans in uniform). In the latter series are orientation films: <u>Prelude to War</u> (54 mins.), <u>The Nazis Strike</u> (41 mins.), <u>Divide and Conquer</u> (83 mins.), <u>The Battle of Britain</u> (55 mins.), <u>The Battle of China</u> (67 mins.), and <u>War Comes to America</u> (67 mins.). Also important are <u>The Negro Soldier</u> (42 mins.) and <u>Know Your Enemy</u>: <u>Japan</u> (63 mins.). Films focusing on battles include <u>The Battle of Midway</u> (18 mins.) and <u>The Battle of San Pietro</u> (33 mins.). All are distributed by the National Audio-Visual Center.

10. <u>The Expanding Conflict: 1940-1941</u> and <u>A World at War: 1942-1945</u> (12 mins. and 16 mins., respectively; provides a global context for the conflict)

11. <u>Negro Soldier</u> (40 mins; VHS. Wartime documentary directed by Frank Capra)

Photographs

<u>A Cartoon History of World War II</u> (39 reproductions), <u>The Rise and Fall Nazi Germany</u> (40 photos), and <u>The Relocation of Japanese-Americans</u> (15 photos), available from Documentary Photo Aids

PART SIX

A RESILIENT PEOPLE

1945–1990

27

Chills and Fever During the Cold War

(1) CHAPTER OUTLINE

Val Lorwin, a State Department employee with 15 years of distinguished government service, is charged by an unnamed accuser of being a Communist and a security risk. After four years of struggle and new accusations, he finally clears himself of the charges before taking up a new career as a labor historian.

Conflicting World Views

> The American Stance
> Soviet Aims
> Cold War Leadership

Origins of the Cold War

> Disillusionment with the USSR
> The Polish Question
> Economic Pressure on the USSR
> Declaring the Cold War

Containing the Soviet Union

> Containment Defined
> The Truman Doctrine
> The Marshall Plan, NATO, and NSC-68
> Containment in the 1950s

American Policy in Asia, the Middle East, and Latin
American

> The Chinese Revolution
> The War in Korea
> Civil War in Vietnam
> The Middle East
> Restricting Revolt in Latin America

Atomic Weapons and the Cold War

> Sharing the Secret of the Bomb
> Nuclear Proliferation
> "Massive Retaliation"

The Cold War at Home

> Truman's Loyalty Program
> The Congressional Loyalty Program
> The Second Red Scare
> The Casualties of Fear

Conclusion: The Cold War in Perspective

(2) SIGNIFICANT THEMES AND HIGHLIGHTS

1. Val Lorwin's struggle reveals the central theme of
   this chapter: the breakdown in relations between the
   Soviet Union and the United States and the domestic
   consequences of the chills and fevers of the Cold
   War. Lorwin was more fortunate than many other
   victims of the paranoiac anti-Communist crusade at
   home.

2. Aside from its ugly domestic effects--loyalty
   programs and the Red Scare--the Cold War thoroughly
   colored all foreign policy decisions of the United
   States after 1945. This chapter describes
   Russian-American relations, the beginnings of the
   Cold War, and U.S. efforts to contain communism in
   Europe, Asia, the Middle East, and Latin America. As
   throughout its history, the United States was
   motivated by an idealistic sense of mission to make
   the world safe for both democracy and American
   capitalism.

3. When both the Soviet Union and the United States
   possessed nuclear weapons capable of destroying the
   world, a troubling and dangerous new element entered
   into the Cold War struggle.

(3) LEARNING GOALS

Familiarity with Basic Knowledge

After reading this chapter, you should be able to:

1. Describe the conflicting political and economic goals of the United States and the USSR for the postwar world, and how these clashing aims launched the Cold War.

2. Define containment and explain the development and meaning of the Truman Doctrine, the Marshall Plan, and NATO.

3. Show how the Chinese Revolution, the Korean War, and the civil war in Vietnam affected U.S. Cold War foreign policy.

4. Name two or three main principles of the Eisenhower-Dulles foreign policy and describe two or three events that tested that policy in Europe, Southeast Asia, the Middle East, and Latin America.

5. Describe the process and effects of nuclear proliferation during the Cold War.

6. Show the relationship between the Cold War and the emergence of internal loyalty programs and the Second Red Scare in the United States.

Practice in Historical Thinking Skills

After reading this chapter, you should be able to:

1. Make a case for both American and Soviet responsibility for the outbreak of the Cold War.

2. Compare and contrast the effectiveness of the Eisenhower-Dulles foreign policy with that of Truman, Marshall, and Acheson.

3. Evaluate the impact of the Cold War on domestic events.

(4) ENRICHMENT IDEAS

1. If you had been living in the United States in 1950, how would you have voted on the questions included in public-opinion polls found in the RTP for this chapter? How would you vote on the same or similar questions today? If there is a change, how do you explain it?

2. Develop a detailed chronology of foreign policy events from 1945 to 1950, showing the actions and reactions by the United States and the Soviet Union. The list should suggest the two nations' mutual responsibility for escalating tensions during the Cold War.

3. Simulate the Cold War in the game Diplomacy or Risk.

Instructor:

4. A lecture (with maps) building on the students' chronology of events between 1945 and 1950 (or 1960) will show clearly the shrinking world and the inevitable involvement of the United States around the globe.

5. Lecture on (and hand out generous excerpts from) Truman's speech introducing the Truman Doctrine. Students could be asked to concentrate on the language Truman used, his description of the crisis, or his candor with the American people. Explore some of the reasons behind Truman's presentation, and assess the long-range diplomatic consequences of this doctrine. This can lead into a discussion of the origins and consequences of the Cold War.

6. A discussion or lecture on the similarities and differences between the Red Scare of the 1920s and McCarthyism can be provocative. The film Point of Order captures the style and perspective of McCarthy in a vivid way for the students.

7. A paper assignment, focused on either a Cold War incident or the McCarthy hearings, that sends students back into the newspapers would help them to assess the mood of the country and encourage them to think about historical interpretation. In what ways is the presentation of this chapter different from or similar to what was written at the time? See Chapters 19 and 20 in Nash, Retracing the Past, Volume Two.

8. A lecture focusing on the contributions of American foreign policy as well as the distinct characteristics of the Truman approach as compared to the Eisenhower approach can be useful.

(5) FURTHER RESOURCES

Documentaries and Films

1. American Foreign Policy: Challenges of Coexistence (24 mins.; made in 1965, focuses on confrontation situation and raises questions of interpretation)

2. American Foreign Policy: Confrontation (1945-1953) (32 mins.; combines commentaries by Chet Huntley and David Brinkley with comments of participants)

3. American Foreign Policy: Containment in Asia (32 mins.; case study of South Vietnam and divided opinion in 1965 about American alternatives)

4. American Foreign Policy: Instrument of Intervention (13 mins.; deals with Latin America)

5. The Truman Years: Truman and the Cold War and Korean War (18 mins. each; shows Truman's part in shaping the postwar world and his own analysis of Cold War rivalry)

6. Charge and Countercharge (43 mins.; army-McCarthy hearings)

7. The Black Soldier (26 mins.; traces the participation of blacks in wartime)

8. Focus on the '40s (58 mins.; made in 1981)

9. An American Ism: Joe McCarthy (85 mins.; follows McCarthy's career, interviews associates and friends as well as opponents)

10. A Crime to Fit the Punishment (46 mins.; investigates events and political atmosphere surrounding the making of a labor film, Salt of the Earth, despite attempts to prevent production of the film)

11. Seeing Red (100 mins.; a film and video view of the passionate commitment and numbing disillusionment of members of the American Communist party from the 1930s to the 1950s)

28

Postwar Growth and Social Change

(1) CHAPTER OUTLINE

Ray Kroc starts the McDonald's drive-in hamburger chain in 1954 and makes a fortune, capitalizing on the conformist suburban American desire for the security and standardization represented by the bland fast-food hamburger. His success symbolizes the fulfillment of one version of the American dream.

Economic Boom

 The Peacetime Economy
 The Corporate World
 The Workers' World
 The Agricultural World
 Population Shifts and the New Suburbs
 Technology Supreme
 The Consumer Culture

Consensus and Conformity

 Conformity in School and Religious Life
 Back to the Kitchen
 Cultural Rebels

Domestic Policy Under Truman and Eisenhower

Reconversion
Postwar Public Policy
Truman Battles a Conservative Congress
The Fair Deal and Its Critics
The Election of Eisenhower
"Modern Republicanism"

The Other America

Poverty amid Affluence
African-Americans and Civil Rights
Integrating the Schools
Black Gains on Other Fronts
Mexican Migrant Laborers
Native Americans

Conclusion: Qualms amid Affluence

(2) SIGNIFICANT THEMES AND HIGHLIGHTS

1. Ray Kroc's success with McDonald's almost perfectly suggests the domestic themes and social emphases of American life in the 1950s--the importance of the automobile, bland fast-food meals, and profitable franchises to standardize life. As symbolized by McDonald's, uniformity, conformity, materialism and suburban security were the hallmarks of America in the 1950s.

2. This triumph of material self-interest was a white middle-class phenomenon. The experience of blacks, Native Americans, and Hispanics showed the limits of economic growth and of social policy in a conservative age.

3. An economic boom in a more highly-structured era of social and technological change dominated the tone of the age. This chapter shows how such social phenomena as television, advertising, the birth rate, studies of sexual behavior, and popular songs, as well as fast-food chains, can be used to understand the character of an age.

(3) LEARNING GOALS

Familiarity with Basic Knowledge

After reading this chapter, you should be able to:

1. Describe the postwar economic boom and its effects in the corporate world, workers' world, and agricultural world.

2. Describe the demographic growth patterns of the United States in the postwar years and state the appeal of suburban living and the automobile for the American people.

3. Give some examples of cultural conformity in the 1950s, particularly on women's lives, and describe the values espoused by cultural rebels.

4. Characterize Truman's challenges as he faced reelection in 1948 and give three reasons why he won.

5. Characterize Eisenhower's philosophy and behavior as president.

6. Describe five economic developments of the 1950s and explain both the importance of the auto industry and the pattern of business concentration.

7. Describe the reasons for the advent of the civil rights movement, and describe black protest and gains in the 1950s.

Practice in Historical Thinking Skills

After reading this chapter, you should be able to:

1. Analyze the social implications of the economic boom and population shifts in postwar American society.

2. Compare and evaluate the Truman and Eisenhower administrations.

3. Assess the gains and losses of groups in "the other America" in the postwar years.

(4) ENRICHMENT IDEAS

1. After working through the songs and questions in the RTP for this chapter, find other popular songs from the 1950s and analyze how they reflect the values, priorities, and concerns of the American people in that decade. Examine song lyrics as if they were poems (admittedly bad ones). Find representative popular songs for the next three decades and analyze them also, finishing with your own time. How has popular music changed? What does this say about changing values among young people in the past 40 years?

2. In addition to the novels cited in the chapter, you might want to read Sylvia Plath's The Bell Jar. In this novel, the heroine is an intelligent student at Smith College who can find no clear sense of direction. How does the plight of the main character reflect some of the themes of this chapter? J. D. Salinger's Catcher in the Rye is an excellent novel in which to explore a young man's anxieties and search for purpose and direction to his life, as is Ralph Ellison's Invisible Man.

3. An interesting exercise that can lead to insights about the past and about your own family focuses on growing up in the 1950s. You can interview one of your parents (even better both, separately) about what it was like to grow up in the decade of the 1950s. How did they spend their leisure time? What was family life like? What kind of music did they listen to? What do they now see as the most important facet of the decade for them? How well do the themes outlined in this chapter seem to fit their experiences? How was their growing up different from that of their parents? Do you see significant differences between the experiences of your mother and your father? How has your own upbringing been the same as or different from that of your parents?

4. Read some of the popular magazines of the period-- Ladies Home Journal or Sports Illustrated. Study both the articles and the advertisements. What can they tell you about values and norms and about the life style of middle-class Americans?

<u>Instructor:</u>

5. Social commentators have been fond of comparing the present generation of college students to the generation of the 1950s. You could have a discussion in which students first create a profile of young people in the 1950s and then compare and contrast the typical 1950s student with themselves.

6. This chapter can be enriched by a lecture or discussion on the civil rights movement, focusing on the reasons why the movement emerged on a national scale in the mid-1950s. Students' understanding of civil rights can be enhanced here by introducing the process and dual thrust of the movement: grass-roots activism by black masses (Montgomery bus boycott) combined with actions--sometimes long delayed--by the (white) federal government (Supreme Court decisions, etc.).

7. Students are enriched--and fascinated--by reading and discussing (or hearing a lecture on) the importance of sports, especially the role of Jackie Robinson, for the rise of civil rights and black pride (see Jules Tygiel, <u>Baseball's Great Experiment: Jackie Robinson and His Legacy</u>).

8. Martin Luther King Jr. can best be understood by being experienced through films (<u>King: Montgomery to Memphis</u>, the first reel), recordings of his speeches and sermons, and studies of his powerful rhetorical style and impact. See Chapter 22 in Nash, <u>Retracing the Past</u>, Volume Two.

(5) FURTHER RESOURCES

Documentaries and Films

1. <u>Truman: A Self-portrait</u> (21 mins.; 1984 film produced by the Truman Centennial Committee and the Smithsonian Institution)

2. <u>The Truman Years: Truman and the Uses of Power</u> (19 mins.; Truman discusses handling of domestic issues)

3. <u>Dwight D. Eisenhower: The Presidential Years</u> (19 mins.; made in 1974, assesses the Eisenhower presidency)

4. <u>With All Deliberate Speed</u> (34 mins.; focuses on Clarendon County, South Carolina, and efforts there to improve black schools)

5. <u>Strange Victory</u> (75 mins.; made in 1948, this film explores the contrast between victory over Nazism and racism at home)

6. <u>Focus on the '50s</u> (58 mins.; made in 1981, shows high points of the decade)

7. <u>Life Goes to the Movies</u>. Parts 3, <u>The Post War Era</u> (20 mins.) and 4, <u>The '50s</u> (28 mins.)

8. <u>The Last Menominee</u> (30 mins.; results of the termination policy for the Menominee Indians)

9. <u>Fundi: The Story of Ella Baker</u> (45 mins.; story of an early leader of the civil rights movement, "mother" to both SCLC and SNCC)

Photographs

<u>Sen. Joe McCarthy vs. Communism</u> (14 photos) and <u>The Rosenberg Atomic Spy Case</u> (17 photos), available from Documentary Photo Aids

29

Politics and Governmental Power

(1) CHAPTER OUTLINE

Ron Kovic was a secure and confident young American boy while growing up on Long Island in the 1950s. His boyhood was filled with baseball, television, and patriotic World War II movies. Inspired by John Wayne and John Kennedy, he answered his country's call to service. On a second tour of duty in Vietnam, a sniper's bullet in the spine sent Kovic home paralyzed from the chest down and filled with despair, anger, and doubts about himself and his country's goodness.

John F. Kennedy and the New Frontier

> The Changing Role of Government
> The Election of 1960
> JFK
> The New Frontier
> Assassination

Lyndon Johnson and the Great Society

> LBJ
> The Great Society in Action
> A Sympathetic Supreme Court
> The Great Society Under Attack

Republican Leadership

> The Election of 1968
> The Nixon Administration
> The Economy Under Nixon
> Watergate
> The Ford Interlude

The Continuing Cold War and Its Consequences

> Kennedy's Confrontations
> Escalation in Vietnam
> Détente

Conclusion: Political Readjustment

(2) SIGNIFICANT THEMES AND HIGHLIGHTS

1. Ron Kovic's individual odyssey from contented confidence to despairing doubt mirrors the course of American politics during the 1960s and 1970s. In a dramatic period of change, the optimistic hopes that the government could solve the nation's domestic and foreign problems, characteristic of the early 1960s under John Kennedy, were replaced by pessimism, doubts, and uncertainty by the mid-1970s. The morality of government as well as its role were questioned as a result of both the Vietnam War and the Watergate crisis.

2. The domestic programs of the 1960s--marked by the liberal welfare assumptions of John Kennedy's New Frontier and Lyndon Johnson's Great Society-- represented a major assault on serious social and economic problems. That they fell far short of their goals raised questions in subsequent Republican administrations over how far government should or would go in providing for the welfare of its citizens.

3. Similarly, the web of United States entanglements and commitments in foreign affairs, most seriously in Vietnam, raised the same kind of redefinition of governmental role occurring on the domestic front.

(3) LEARNING GOALS

Familiarity with Basic Knowledge

After reading this chapter, you should be able to:

1. Define the meaning of John Kennedy's "New Frontier" and describe the tone, achievements, and failures of his administration.

2. Define Lyndon Johnson's "Great Society" and describe how well it achieved or failed to achieve its goals.

3. Describe the goals and styles of leadership under the Republican administrations of Richard Nixon and Gerald Ford.

4. Tell the story of the presidential elections of 1960, 1968, and 1972, including the story of Watergate.

5. Identify the arguments for and against strong assertions of governmental power in the 1960s and 1970s.

6. Outline the major events and significance of the confrontations in Cuba under Kennedy, the war in Vietnam under Johnson and Nixon, and the improvement of relations with China and the USSR under Nixon.

Practice in Historical Thinking Skills

After reading this chapter, you should be able to:

1. Analyze the goals, styles, achievements, and limitations of the presidential administrations of Kennedy, Johnson, and Nixon.

2. Evaluate the place of the Vietnam War in American history.

3. Explain and defend, with historical examples, your own position on the proper role of the federal government in domestic and foreign affairs in this changing world.

(4) ENRICHMENT IDEAS

1. After analyzing the Watergate cartoons in the RTP for
    the chapter, find other cartoons by Tony Auth,
    Herblock, and Jules Feiffer, as well as by Garry
    Trudeau ("Doonesbury") and Charles Schultz
    ("Peanuts"), and explore how they reflect other
    aspects of American life in the 1970s. Look
    particularly for cartoons about social phenomena: the
    women's movement, civil rights, the counterculture
    and the generation gap, the environmental and
    consumer movements, and the human potential movement.

2. Interview people about their recollections of and
    reactions to Watergate, the Nixon administration, and
    the change in social mood from the intense public
    activism of the 1960s to the inward-looking privatism
    of the 1970s. Would they agree with that
    description? If not, how do they explain it?

Instructor:

3. A family history assignment, including oral
    interviews, is especially appropriate for this
    chapter, focusing, if you wish, on the war's impact
    or on responses to the counterculture and so on.
    Students could also research the events of the 1960s
    on their own campus, again relying on oral interviews
    as well as on campus archives and student newspapers.

4. Students could be asked to interview two or three
    people, not necessarily family members, about certain
    foreign policy events of the period: Cuban missile
    crisis, Vietnam War, Bay of Pigs. The same
    assignment could be directed at domestic events.
    After the interviews, students could be asked to
    contrast the views of the events gained from the
    interviews to the general interpretation provided by
    the chapter. What accounts for the similarities and
    differences between the two?

5. LBJ and Nixon make fascinating subjects for study.
    See Chaper 24 in Nash, Retracing the Past, Volume
    Two.

(5) FURTHER RESOURCES

Documentaries and Films

1. <u>Cuba: Bay of Pigs</u> (29 mins.; NBC White Paper report by Chet Huntley)

2. <u>One Week in October</u> (30 mins.; made in 1969, focuses on Cuban missile crisis)

3. <u>Who Invited Us?</u> (60 mins.; places intervention in Latin America and elsewhere in the context of American actions throughout the twentieth century)

4. <u>Hearts and Minds</u> (110 mins.; critique of involvement in Vietnam and exploration of cultural reasons for it)

5. <u>The End of the Ho Chi Minh Trail</u> (89 mins.; videocassette focusing on impact of war in South and North Vietnam and in the United States)

6. <u>The Age of Kennedy</u>. Part 2, <u>The Presidency</u> (50 mins.; narrated by Chet Huntley and made for NBC)

7. <u>Focus on 1960-1964: The Kennedy Years</u>, and <u>Focus on 1965-1969: The Angry Years</u> (58 mins. each)

8. <u>The Fabulous 60's</u> (a VHS year-by-year series on the 1960s; each 60 mins.)

9. <u>JFK Remembered</u> (55 mins; a VHS production, made in 1988 and hosted by Peter Jennings)

10. <u>Vietnam: the War at Home</u> (100 mins; VHS contrasts on student activities against the war)

11. <u>America Against Itself</u> (45 mins; a treatment of the Democratic Convention of 1968)

12. <u>Dear America: Letters Home from Vietnam</u> (87 mins; video format. Letters from soldiers as well as previously unreleased footage and music of the era)

13. <u>The Selling of the Pentagon</u> (50 mins.)

14. <u>Vietnam: A Historical Documentary</u> (57 mins.; covers 1950-1975; as the most photographed war, Walter Cronkite asks, "What did it add up to?")

15. <u>Nixon: From Checkers to Watergate</u> (20 mins.)

16. <u>An Essay on Watergate</u> (60 mins.; Bill Moyer's attempt to understand and put in perspective the events of Watergate)

Photographs

<u>The Negro Experience in America</u> (49 photos), <u>The Cuban Missile Crisis</u> (14 photos), and <u>The Migrant Farm Workers</u> (20 photos), available from Documentary Photo Aids.

<u>Watergate: A Cartoon History</u> (34 reproductions), available from Documentary Photo Aids.

30

The Struggle for Social Reform

(1) CHAPTER OUTLINE

Ann Clarke, born Antonina Rose Rumore, put her Lower
East Side, New York City, Italian working-class origins
behind her as she went to California and married a
college-educated chemist. After 15 years of faithful
devotion to her husband and three children, she enrolled in
college. Not without considerable conflict and worries,
especially over her "sixties"-style children, Ann managed to
complete a degree and start a career of her own as a
teacher.

The Black Struggle for Equality

  Confrontation
  Kennedy's Response
  Civil Rights Under Johnson
  Black Power Challenges Liberal Reform
  "Southern Strategy" and Showdown on Civil Rights

The Women's Movement

  Attacking the Feminine Mystique
  Feminism at High Tide

Hispanic Rights

  César Chávez and the Politics of Confrontation

Native American Protest

    Tribal Voices
    Indian Activism
    Government Response

Social and Cultural Protest

    The Student Movement
    The Counterculture
    Environment and Consumer Movements
    Countercurrents of Self

Conclusion: Extending the American Dream

(2) SIGNIFICANT THEMES AND HIGHLIGHTS

1. The changes Ann Clarke went through typifies those of millions of other women in the 1960s and 1970s. Traumatic alterations in traditional patterns of women's experience and family life grew out of and compounded the struggles for social reform that marked the 1960s and early 1970s.

2. The dominant reform movement of the era was the black struggle for equality. This chapter traces that struggle from the civil rights movement of the early sixties under Martin Luther King, Jr. to the black power movement of the late sixties inspired by the martyred Malcolm X. By the 1970s, the Nixon administration demonstrated the lessening of concern among white Americans for black equality and rights.

3. The black struggle inspired similar movements to recognize the voices and rights for women, Hispanics, and Native Americans, as well as those speaking for the environment and the consumer.

4. Resistance to these movements by the established order and older generations, along with the escalating war in Vietnam, fed both the idealism and disillusionment of young people, who embraced political radicalism and adopted new standards of cultural taste and personal behavior.

(3) LEARNING GOALS

Familiarity with Basic Knowledge

After reading this chapter, you should be able to:

1. Describe the major confrontations over civil rights in the 1960s and state Kennedy's, Johnson's, and Nixon's responses to the black struggle for equality.

2. Explain the reasons for the shift in the civil rights movement from its nonviolent phase to the black power militancy of the late sixties.

3. State the major goals of feminist leaders and show the similarities between the women's and civil rights movements.

4. Describe the efforts of Hispanic and Native American leaders and groups to improve their position and quality of life, and show how these movements also were patterned on the black experience.

5. Explain the reasons for the student protest movement and characterize the values of the counterculture.

6. Describe the environmental and consumer protection movements.

Practice in Historical Thinking Skills

After reading this chapter, you should be able to:

1. Analyze and evaluate the reasons for and wisdom of the shift in the black struggle from nonviolent direct action to black power.

2. Discuss the influence of the black movement for equality and rights on those by women, Hispanics, and Native Americans.

3. Describe and evaluate the influence of youth culture in recent American life.

(4) ENRICHMENT IDEAS

1. The RTP suggests the power of television to shape
    American views and responses to events. Television
    also conveyed the norms of the period and captured
    some of the confusion and anger that changing values
    and tastes could generate. You may be able to see
    some reruns of programs from the 1960s; if so, look
    for evidence of social values, for suggestions of
    gender and age norms, for signs of challenges to
    familiar ways of thought and action, and even for
    typical prime-time programming that shows another
    side to the 1960s than protest.

2. There are so many possibilities for enriching the
    study of the 1960s that only a few need be suggested
    here: feature films (The Graduate, Dr. Strangelove,
    Bonnie and Clyde, Easy Rider, etc.); novels (Joseph
    Heller, Catch-22; Ken Kesey, One Flew over the
    Cuckoo's Nest; Peter Tauber, The Last Best Hope;
    Marge Piercy, Small Changes; etc.); rock and folk
    music (the Beatles; the Rolling Stones; Peter, Paul
    and Mary; etc.). Your imagination can come into full
    play in researching and reliving this recent and
    memorable decade.

3. As you approach the present, issues of interpretation
    (or lack of interpretation) become more pressing and
    controversial. Some historians argue that interpret-
    ing the recent past is impossible and should be
    avoided, while others insist that providing an
    interpretive understanding of contemporary history is
    a crucial responsibility. To what extent does this
    chapter have an interpretation? Does it correspond
    to your view or that of your parents?

Instructor:

4. Folk and rock music offer many possibilities, both in
    terms of the lyrics and the music itself. Students
    are, of course, familiar with much of the music but
    may well not understand the relation of music to the
    events described in the chapter. Most teachers have
    their own musical favorites from the 1960s that will
    interest students.

5. Assignments dealing with some of the phenomena of the
    "generation gap" can be fruitful. Students can be
    asked to compare their own values, attitudes, and
    activities with those of their parents. What

differences exist between themselves and their parents? How do these differences compare to those their parents remember having with _their_ parents? How has the "generation gap" changed from the 1960s, if at all?

6. _I Have a Dream_ (33 mins.) is an excellent and provocative film on Martin Luther King's career. _King: Montgomery to Memphis_ (103 mins.) is a powerful vehicle for discussion, as are films and records capturing the voice and career of Malcolm X (_El-Hajj Malik El-Shabazz_, 58 mins., "Message to the Grass-roots.") _The '60s_ (15 mins.) is a good short introduction to the period, mainly in the form of music and images.

7. Lectures can be enriched with slides of the 1960s videotapes of television broadcasts, and the two-record set _Sounds of the Sixties,_ narrated by Walter Cronkite, or _Voices of the Civil Rights Movement: Black American Freedom Songs, 1960-66,_ issued by the Smithsonian Institution. Innovative and energetic teachers might experiment with synchronized slide-tape presentations for full emotional and dramatic impact of the stirring events of this decade (civil rights songs or King's speeches with slides of the movement, for example, or Vietnam songs and slides, how music reflected the decade, or the four assassinations).

(5) FURTHER RESOURCES

Documentaries and Films

1. _Oh Freedom! The Story of the Civil Rights Movement_ (26 mins.; narrated by Reverend Andrew Young, deals with civil rights and black power)

2. _A Day to Remember: August 28, 1963_ (29 mins.; videocassette focuses on the march on Washington and has interviews with some of principal figures)

3. _My Childhood: Hubert Humphrey's South Dakota and James Baldwin's Harlem_ (51 mins.; made in 1964, highlights the different experiences of white and black Americans)

4. _A Stroke of the Pen: Dimensions of a Presidential Decision_ (16 mins.: asks what viewer would do if in

Kennedy's place and shows the complexities of civil rights)

5. <u>1968: A Look for New Meanings</u>. Part 1, <u>Viet Nam: The Television War;</u> 2, <u>The Black Movement;</u> 3, <u>Student Protesters;</u> and 4, <u>The Battle of Chicago</u> (each 30 mins.)

6. <u>Mississippi Summer</u> (58 min.; an award winner focusing on the background to and events of the summer of 1964)

7. <u>Should the Equal Rights Amendment Be Ratified?</u> (59 mins.; videocassette featuring Eleanor Smeal of NOW and Phyllis Schlafly)

8. <u>Hunger in America</u> (51 mins.; shows hunger among Mexican-Americans in Texas, Indians in Arizona, blacks in Alabama, and sharecroppers in Virginia)

9. <u>El Mojado</u> (The Wetback) (20 mins.; made in 1974, shows the plight of undocumented Mexican workers trying to cross into the United States)

10. <u>Equality</u> (60 mins.; award-winning film made in 1976 featuring interviews with Americans in all walks of life)

11. <u>The War at Home</u> (100 mins.; traces the antiwar movement)

12. <u>Protest on the Campus: Columbia University, 1968</u> (15 mins.)

13. <u>Underground</u> (88 mins.; documentary on the Weather Underground organization and political activism in the 1960s and 1970s)

14. <u>Confrontation at Kent State</u> (45 mins.; put together by students at Kent State University and friends and family of those killed there)

15. <u>The American Wilderness</u> (50 mins.; the wilderness seen as an irreplaceable resource)

31

The United States Since 1976: Redefining the American Dream

(1) CHAPTER OUTLINE

Andy Hjelmeland and Jerry Espinoza, both men in their mid-forties, found themselves out of work in the early 1980s. Although both were confident that they would soon find another job, changed economic circumstances (and, for Jerry, discrimination) made their search for employment futile. Their self-esteem suffered. Their personal depression deepened as they concluded that their government was indifferent to their woes.

The Disordered Economy

    Regional Difficulties
    Improvement and Instability
    Labor in Transition
    Trouble on the Farm

The Demographic Transformation

    American Society in 1980
    The New Pilgrims
    Growing Up
    Growing Old
    The New Students

The Continuing Struggle for Equality

    Consolidating Feminist Gains

The Continuing Significance of Race
The First Americans Still Last

The New Reformers

Gay Liberation
Consumer and Environmental Activism
Vietnam Veterans
Religious Fundamentalism

Carter, Reagan, and Beyond

The Election of 1976
Human Rights Diplomacy
Carter's Domestic Program
Reagan's Electoral Victories
Reagan in Office
Reviving the Cold War
Dismantling the Welfare State
The Election of 1988

Conclusion: The Recent Past in Perspective

(2) SIGNIFICANT THEMES AND HIGHLIGHTS

1. The dominant theme of this latest chapter in American history is that of a disordered economy. America's economic woes colored politics and policy as well as the lives of people like Andy Hjelmeland and Jerry Espinoza. For both men, and for many other Americans, the decade of the 1980s brought economic instability and particular troubles to farmers, blue-collar workers, and women heading single-parent families.

2. Changing demographic trends gave American society a particular character in the 1970s and 1980s. Americans were older, more often divorced, and more often living in nontraditional households. Immigrants from Latin America and the Far East introduced new pilgrims into the mosaic of the American people.

3. In the continuing effort to fulfill the American dream for all people, blacks, women, and other groups that had won fragile gains in the previous 15 years continued to press for change. New reformers joined the attempt to transform American life.

4. The political mood of the country was far less
    sympathetic to reform than had been true in the
    recent past. More concerned with reestablishing U.S.
    prestige in foreign affairs and in weakening domestic
    welfare programs, Reagan presided over a return of
    prosperity to American society, although unevenly
    experienced, and passed on a troubling list of
    difficult problems to his successor, George Bush.

(3) LEARNING GOALS

Familiarity with Basic Knowledge

After reading this chapter, you should be able to:

1. Describe the disordered economy of the 1980s,
    indicating which segments of the population have done
    well and which have not.

2. Identify four important recent demographic character-
    istics of American society and explain what
    consequences each has had.

3. Characterize the gains and losses made by women,
    blacks, Hispanics, and Native Americans in the 1980s.

4. Describe the "new reformers" and their goals.

5. Show how Reagan's political philosophy was reflected
    in domestic and foreign policy while president.

Practice in Historical Thinking Skills

After reading this chapter, you should be able to:

1. Understand how recent policy toward Latin America and
    the Middle East is both a continuation of policies
    developed before World War II and an extension of the
    Cold War.

2. Evaluate the ways in which the administration of
    Ronald Reagan represented a shift away from the
    domestic policies of the country since the New Deal.

3. Identify and analyze the enduring continuities and
    tensions in the American people that persist in our
    lives today.

(4) ENRICHMENT IDEAS

1. Autobiographies--your own as well as those by
    Franklin, Stanton, Malcolm X, and others--reveal the
    story of the American people. An autobiography, as
    Thoreau's Walden suggests, need not, in fact, cannot
    "cover" one's entire life. Like historians,
    autobiographers face problems of sources, selection,
    embellishment, and interpretation. The following
    short exercise will reveal these problems, as well as
    some insights into yourself.

    First, research and write (in two pages) the story of
    your life for a month's time three years ago. This
    will no doubt raise problems primarily of sources--
    how to find out what you were doing, what happened
    during that month. Writing about your life will also
    raise issues of embellishment as you seek to describe
    and maybe even to interpret those half-remembered
    high school horrors. Second, research and write (in
    two pages) the story of your life last week. Note
    that your primary problem here is not memory and
    sources but selection. How will you decide which
    among the hundreds of facts you know about your life
    last week should be selected? Perhaps an
    interpretive framework, a theme, or a thesis point of
    view will help.

    Conclude your autobiography with one paragraph that
    connects or shows the relationship between the you of
    three years ago and the you of last week. The con
    necting theme might be found in a significant
    continuity, in a change, or in something else, but
    whatever it is, it will suggest the importance of
    interpretation in transforming a catalog of factual
    events into a story. In writing this paper about
    your own life, you are, in the highest sense, doing
    history.

2. This chapter covers the recent past, which is acces-
    sible to you in a way that other periods are not. You
    might want to think about the way in which the
    chapter treats these years. Would you characterize
    them in the same way? What would you consider to be
    the greatest problems of the recent past? The most
    positive features? How have the currents of recent
    years affected your family and your own hopes and
    dreams?

3. Assess the "Reagan Revolution."

178

<u>Instructor:</u>

4. Use your own ideas.

(5) FURTHER RESOURCES

Documentaries and Films

1. <u>The Unsung Soldiers</u> (26 mins.; readjustment of
    Vietnam veterans)

2. <u>Danger: Radioactive Waste</u> (60 mins.; 1977 NBC report)

3. <u>Peanuts to the Presidency</u> (30 mins.; Jimmy Carter)

4. <u>The Farm</u> (24 mins.; made in 1976, compares
    agricultural life in the 1970s to that of the
    eighteenth century)

5. <u>The Battle of Westlands</u> (59 mins.; 1980 film showing
    struggle of small family farmers against
    agribusiness)

6. <u>Focus on the Seventies: Science and Technology</u> (20
    mins., shows the country reevaluating itself)

7. <u>Down and Out in America</u> (57 mins.; VHS. Won the
    academy award as the best documentary in 1986)

8. <u>The Reagan Years: In Pursuit of the American Dream</u>
    (77 mins.; VHS. Made in 1988, focusing on Reagan's
    two terms in office)

9. <u>The Collective: Fifteen Years Later</u> (60 mins.; VHS
    format. A look at radicals of the 1970s)

10. <u>Children of Labor: A Finnish-American History</u> (55
    mins.; three generations of working-class Americans)

11. <u>Becoming American: The Odyssey of a Refugee Family</u>
    (30 mins.; a Laotian family's difficult and heroic
    resettlement in Seattle)

12. <u>Quilts in Women's Lives</u> (28 mins.; a wonderful
    portrayal of women's artistic expression of the
    meaning of their lives)

Selected Addresses of Film Distributors and
Other Audiovisual Materials

ACI Productions
35 West 45th Street
New York, NY 10036

Amalgamated Clothing Workers of America
AFL-CIO
15 Union Square
New York, NY 10003

Ambrose Video Publishers, Inc.
381 Park Ave. South, Suite 1601
New York, NY 10016

Anti-Defamation League of B'Nai B'Rith
315 Lexington Avenue
New York, NY 10016

Audio Brandon Film Library
34 Macquestan Parkway South
Mount Vernon, NY 10550

Audio-Forum
145 East 49th Street
New York, NY 10017

Audio Learning, Inc.
44 Parkway West
Mount Vernon, NY 10552

BFA Educational Media
2211 Michigan Avenue
Santa Monica, CA 90404

California Newsreel
630 Natoma St.
San Francisco, CA 94103

Carousel Films
1501 Broadway, Suite 1503
New York, NY 10036

The Cinema Guild
1697 Broadway
New York, NY 10019

Colonial Williamsburg Foundation
A.V. Distribution Center
Box C
Williamsburg, VA 23185

Coronet/MTI Film & Video
108 Wilmot Road
Deerfield, IL 60015

Documentary Photo Aids, Inc.
P.O. Box 956
Mount Dora, FL 32757

Educational Audio Visual
29 Marble Avenue
Pleasantville, NY 10570

Encyclopaedia Britannica Educational Corporation
425 North Michigan Avenue
Chicago, IL 60611

Filmakers Library
133 East 58th Street
New York, NY 10022

Films, Inc.
733 Green Bay Road
Wilmette, IL 60019

Films for the Humanities
P.O. Box 2053
Princeton, NJ 08543

Hearst Metrotone News
450 West 56th Street
New York, NY 10019

Indiana University
Audio Visual Center
Bloomington, IN 47401

Instructional Resources Corporation
American History Slide Collection
1819 Bay Ridge Avenue
Annapolis, MD 21403

International Film Bureau
332 South Michigan Avenue
Chicago, IL 60604

IQ Films
689 Fifth Avenue
New York, NY 10022

Learning Corporation of America
711 Fifth Avenue
New York, NY 10022
McGraw-Hill Films
110 Fifteenth Street
Del Mar, CA 92014

National Audio-Visual Center
National Archives and Records Service
General Services Administration
Reference Section DL
Washington, DC 20409

New Day Films
22 Riverview Drive
Wayne, NJ 07470

Pacifica Tape Library
5316 Venice Boulevard
Los Angeles, CA 90019

PBS Video
475 L'Enfant Plaza, SW
Washington, DC 20024

Phoenix Films & Videos
468 Park Avenue South
New York, NY 10016

Prentice-Hall Media
150 White Plains Road
Tarrytown, NY 10591

Pyramid Film Productions
P.O. Box 1048
Santa Monica, CA 90406

Shell Film Library
1433 Sadlier Circle West Drive
Indianapolis, IN 46239

Teaching Film Custodians
25 West 43rd Street
New York, NY 10036

Time-Life Multimedia
Room 32-48
Time and Life Building
Rockefeller Center
New York, NY 10020

University of Illinois
Visual Aids Service
1325 South Oak Street
Champaign, IL 61820

Women's Labor History
Film Project
1735 New Hampshire Avenue
Washington, DC 20009

REFERENCES ON TEACHING HISTORY

Two journals, The History Teacher (published quarterly by the Society for History Education) and Teaching History, are the two most indispensable sources for ideas on teaching American History, each containing useful articles on classroom teaching techniques, historiography and reviews of traditional monographs, textbooks, films, and other media for teaching. All teachers of American history will find it worthwhile to look through back issues and to subscribe.

> The History Teacher
> California State University
> 1250 Bellflower Boulevard
> Long Beach, CA 90840
>
> Teaching History: A Journal of Methods
> Division of Social Sciences
> Emporia State University
> Emporia, KS 66801

Other very helpful articles on teaching history (although mixed with articles on other fields and all aspects of higher education) can be found in Change Magazine and College Teaching, published by

> Heldref Publications
> 4000 Albermarle Street, NW
> Washington, DC 20016

Another small organization devoted to excellence and innovation in teaching history is the Committee on History in the Classroom (CHC). For membership and a newsletter, contact

> Dr. Gordon Mork
> Department of History
> University Hall
> Purdue University
> West Lafayette, IN 47907

Both major professional organizations, although primarily serving scholarship, publish pamphlets related to teaching as well as useful articles on teaching in their newsletters and supplements. The AHA Teaching Division is more active in promoting the importance of teaching at the college and university levels than the OAH, which regards pedagogy, as distinct from curriculum development, as appropriate only for secondary teachers.

American Historical Association publications are available from

> Publications Sales Department
> American Historical Association
> 400 A Street, SE
> Washington, DC 20003

These include

> The Introductory History Course: Six Models, ed. Kevin Reilly
> Studying History: An Introduction to Method and Structure, Paul Ward
> Teaching Afro-American History, Robert L. Harris, Jr.
> The Peopling of America: Perspectives on Immigration, Franklin A. Jackson
> Teaching History with Film, John E. O'Connor and Martin A. Jackson

OAH Publications are available from

> Organization of American Historians
> 112 North Bryan Street
> Bloomington, IN 47401

These include

> American History Through Film
> Restoring Women to History: Western Civilization I and II
> Restoring Women to History: U.S. History I and II
> Sport History in the United States: An Overview
> Teaching Public History to Undergraduates
> Computer Applications for Historians (OAH Newsletter Special Supplement, Nov. 1984, with updates)

Also available from OAH is History in Context, a thorough bibliography "about the teaching of history and trends in higher education," compiled and edited by William H. A. Williams (1986). In addition to the Williams collection, the following is a brief bibliography of other sources on teaching and active learning, some focused specifically on American history and some on teaching and learning generally. There are many effective strategies for active inquiry in the study of American history in these readings.

1. Botein, Stephen, et al. eds., <u>Experiments in History Teaching</u> (Cambridge, MA: Harvard-Danforth Center for Teaching and Learning, 1977). Terrific innovative ideas, mostly for assignments and class projects.

2. Cuban, Larry, <u>Teachers and Machines: The Classroom Use of Technology</u> (New York: Columbia Teachers College Press, 1985).

3. Davidson, James W., and Mark Lytle, <u>After the Fact: The Art of Historical Detection</u>, 2d ed. (NY: Alfred Knopf, 1986).

4. Dean, David, "Turning on Clio: A Budget-conscious Approach to Using Media in American History Classes," <u>Social Studies Journal</u> 6 (Spring 1977):14-17.

5. Degler, Carl, "What the Woman's Movement Has Done to American History," <u>Soundings</u> 64 (Winter 1981):403-21.

6. Eble, Kenneth, <u>The Aims of College Teaching</u> (San Francisco: Jossey-Bass, 1983).

7. Eble, Kenneth, <u>The Craft of Teaching</u>, 2d ed. (San Francisco: Jossey-Bass, 1988).

8. Ericksen, Stanford, <u>The Essence of Good Teaching: Helping Students Learn and Remember What They Learn</u> (San Francisco: Jossey-Bass, 1984).

9. Fuhrmann, Barbara Schneider, and Anthony F. Grasha, <u>A Practical Handbook for College Teachers</u> (Boston: Little Brown, 1983). A thorough overview, full of useful exercises and ideas.

10. Furay, Conal, and Michael J. Salevouris, <u>The Methods and Skills of History: A Practical Guide</u> (Arlington Heights, IL: Harlan Davidson, 1987).

11. Gullette, Margaret Morganroth, ed., <u>The Art and Craft of Teaching</u> (Cambridge, MA: Harvard University Press, 1984). Practical essays from the Harvard-Danforth Center for Teaching and Learning.

12. Indochina Curriculum Group, <u>The Vietnam Era: A Guide to Teaching Resources</u> (Cambridge, MA, 1978). See also <u>Vietnam, A Teacher's Guide</u>, <u>Focus on Asian Studies</u> (Fall, 1983).

13. Katz, Joseph, ed., Teaching As Though Students Mattered. New Directions for Teaching and Learning Publication No. 21 (San Francisco: Jossey-Bass, 1985).

14. Levy, Todd, and Donna Collins Krasnow, A Guidebook for Teaching United States History: Earliest Times to the Civil War (vol. 1) and Mid-Nineteenth Century to the Present (vol. 2) (Boston: Allyn & Bacon, 1979).

15. Marsh, Sheila Johnson, comp. U.S. History: A Media Bibliography. Bibliographic Series No. 21. (Sacramento: California State University Library, 1978).

16. McKeachie, Wilbert J., Teaching Tips: A Guidebook for the Beginning College Teacher, 7th ed. (Lexington, MA: D.C. Heath, 1978).

17. Scholl, Stephen C., and Sandra Inglis, eds., Teaching in Higher Education: Readings for Faculty (Columbus: Ohio Boad of Regents, 1977).

18. Stoler, Mark, and Marshall True, Explorations in American History: A Skills Approach (NY: Alfred Knopf, 1987).

19. Watts, Jim, and Allen F. Davis, Generations: Your Family in Modern American History, 3d ed. (New York: Knopf, 1983).

20. Wayland, John, How to Teach American History: A Handbook for Teachers and Students (New York: Macmillan, 1914). An old classic, still full of good sensible advice on pedagogy, although outdated in examples and references.

21. Wheeler, William B., and Susan Becker, Discovering the American Past: A Look at the Evidence, 2 Vols. (NY: Houghton Mifflin, 1986).

College Teaching is published by Heldref Publications, 4000 Albemarle St., N.W., Washington, DC 20016.

Drawings by Jim Hull

The Lively Lecture—8 Variations

PETER J. FREDERICK

> The lecture system to classes of hundreds, which was very much that of the twelfth century, suited Adams not at all. Barred from philosophy and bored by facts, he wanted to teach his students something not wholly useless.
>
> —*The Education of Henry Adams*

The recent flurry of criticisms of higher education, although focusing on an integrated core curriculum and the development of fundamental competencies, all exhort professors and those who administer the faculty reward system to pay more attention to teaching and learning. This means, among other things, increasing faculty "engagement" and interaction with students (especially in the first years of college), developing higher order cognitive and affective capabilities in students, and promoting more active student "involvement" in their own learning.[1] Since both common sense and educational research indicate that these goals are more readily achieved in smaller rather than larger classes, a likely target of these calls for reform is the lecture.

Criticism of the Lecture

Although the *lektor* has been the primary medium of college and university instruction since the middle ages,

---

Studies on attention span suggest that after 15 or 20 minutes the lecture loses its effectiveness even in transmitting information.

---

in recent years it has been under assault not only by distinguished educational panels but also by student protestors, learning theorists, faculty development consultants, and even by (some) tenure and promotion committees. Faculty members have been bombarded with messages to lecture less and to use discussion and other innovative participatory methods of teaching more.

In the sixth edition of his influential book, *Teaching Tips*, Wilbert J. McKeachie concluded that although lectures are "sometimes an effective way of communicating information," he had "a suspicion, . . . supported by bits of evidence, that other methods of teach-

The author is a professor of history and chair, Division of Social Sciences, at Wabash College in Crawfordsville, Indiana. The drawings were made by Jim Hull to accompany a demonstration/discussion by the author on the ideas in this article. That presentation was sponsored by the Teaching Resources Center at Indiana University in Bloomington.

ing may be more effective than lecturing in achieving some of the higher level cognitive and attitudinal objectives."[2] Reflecting a decade of further studies, Bette LaSere Erickson and Glenn R. Erickson emphatically state that "the lecture is less effective than other methods when instructional goals involve the application of information, the development of thinking skills, or the modification of attitudes."[3]

Attention span studies, for example, suggest that after 15 or 20 minutes the lecture loses its effectiveness even in transmitting information. Students, of course, routinely respond that lectures are "boring" and "worthless." Thus, as Henry Adams suspected 80 years ago, if a teacher wants to avoid being "wholly useless," it is best not to lecture.

Justification of the Lecture

Despite all the criticism, however, the lecture has withstood all assaults on its old, yellowed walls, standing up under the siege with battered but enduring strength. The onslaught has done more to cause faculty discomfort and guilt than actually to change practices. From within the safety of the old walls of tenure, tradi-

---

I'd like to try some new ideas, but I can't—I have 300 students in the class, you know.

---

tion, and expediency, faculty members continue to lecture. Only a tone of defensiveness hints at the battle outside. "I'd like to do less lecturing, but I've got too much to cover." Or, "that's all right for you but I have to lecture in my field." Or, "I'd like to try some new ideas, but I can't—I have 300 students in the class, you know." As salvos of rhetoric and reports fly back and forth across the parapets, life in the classroom goes on much as before. Most college professors, even those like myself who advocate a decentralized classroom, still spend more class hours "lecturing" than anything else.

For some good reasons. Other than the expediency of economy of scale, there are many reasonable justifications of the well-prepared, clearly organized, and dynamically delivered lecture. When done well, the best lectures:

- impart new information
- explain, clarify and organize difficult concepts
- model a creative mind at work or the problem-solving process

- analyze and show relationships among seemingly dissimilar ideas
- inspire a reverence for learning
- challenge beliefs and habits of thinking, and
- breed enthusiasm and motivation for further study.

To hear a good lecture is an inspiring experience. We leave with our imagination broadened and our interest piqued; we find ourselves entertained, prodded, and illuminated in turn. What evokes our response is an intricate blend of qualities. The lecture must have sufficient intellectual content to challenge us. . . . Like a dramatic monologue, it engages our emotions and keeps them in play, thanks to frequent shifts in mood and intensity. It mixes humor and erudition, and gives us a sense of the personal involvement of the lecturer . . .[4]

In hearing a lecture like this, Henry Adams notwithstanding, students receive much more than useless facts. Such a lecture, as Emerson said in the "American Scholar" address in 1837, aims "not to drill, but to . . . set the hearts of youth on flame." Ideally, there is engagement, excitement, and intense interaction, albeit passively experienced by students, in the act of listening and recording notes during an inspiring lecture.

In battles over the lecture method, both sides err in holding up a single stereotyped image. Defenders of the lecture usually cite the fiery and inspiring version described above, acknowledging, however, that "in practice . . . too few lectures attain this ideal."[5] Critics paint a dreary picture of the stodgy old pedant (or an uninspiring nervous young one) listlessly mumbling overly long and obtuse sentences read from crumbling, yellowed (or freshly word-processed) notes. Doubtless there are both important facts and gems of wisdom in Professor Mumble's tired words, but they are lost on most students who tune out early to fantasize last night's winning jump shot or the coming weekend's party. At its best, the lecture ends five minutes early as the professor asks, "Are there any questions?" There usually are not.

Neither image of the lecture serves us well. We need, I believe, to redefine the "lecture" in order to achieve the kind of involvement educators have agreed enhances student learning. The purpose of this essay is to suggest several such variations. Although disparate in approach, each variation is motivational; each imparts information; each engages students actively. It is my intention to show that interactive student participation is possible even in the traditional setting of large mass lecture classes in dimly lit halls with tiered rows of immovable seats bolted to the floor.

Other than the obvious importance of content mastery, traditional advice about giving lectures applies to each of the different forms described here. Objectives should be clearly stated and written down on the board with an outline of major topics to be "covered." One should only make two or three major points in any given class, using several focused examples or experiences to illustrate each main idea. Students should be given specific assignments to practice their mastery of these ideas. Teachers should be sensitive to their audience, aware of its energy level, and prepared to adapt the level and form of presentation accordingly, varying the format for different class periods and often even within one period.[6]

Importance of Variety

There is no moment more important than when a professor decides—given a wide array of pedagogical variations from which to choose—that for *these* particular primary and secondary goals for *this* particular class period, *these* particular teaching and learning methods make the most sense. For example, if a new topic is to be introduced, the teacher might either deliver a traditional lecture filled with overarching themes and necessary groundwork information or present an emotionally charged film or multi-media show to arouse interest in the new topic. Or, if students' energy and enthusiasm have been noticeably declining, a teacher will want to structure a way of getting student participation and feedback in order to understand what they are thinking and feeling. Or, if a recent examination has revealed a widespread deficiency in some competency, a class period should be devoted to giving students either a model of or practice in that skill.

Deciding which goal and method is most appropriate for any given class—especially when recognizing that students have different learning styles and are at different stages of cognitive and moral development—is a vitally crucial moment for a teacher's effectiveness in enhancing student learning.

As different students learn from diverse approaches, so also are there diverse ways to be a "good" teacher. The point is to select that style most consistent with one's personality. Students are not fooled when we try to be something other than what we are. But at the same time, since we seek to stretch the ways students learn, they appreciate our openly avowed efforts to expand the ways we teach, even in ways we might initially find uncomfortable. It is in this spirit of guarded but willing experimentation that I hope we will approach these eight variations of a lecture.

1. The Exquisite Oral Essay

This is the traditional lecture, executed with the kind of excellence to which we all aspire—and once in a while achieve. The oral essay is a final polished work which skillfully treats a single intellectual question or problem. It has unity: the topic is introduced, illustrated, and concluded within fifty minutes; it does not spill over to the following Wednesday. Thus, the single class period

is an "intellectual experience" for the students as they listen in awe to the professor's "perfect" presentation. The purpose of this kind of lecture is not only to convey substantive information but also to demonstrate the professor doing well the job of professing. Students are treated to "a window on the teacher's mind," watching with much the same intensity that one has when observing an unusually skillful pianist or salesman. Our courses, no doubt, should include some of these performances, but not to the exclusion of other approaches. Oral essays reduce students to the role of passive auditors, at best engaged in an "internal dialogue," as David Bergman puts it, with the professor.[7] Although the oral essay is inspirationally masterful, the students witness a finished product, not the process.

2. The Participatory Lecture

Would it not be more instructive if students could observe, or better yet participate in, the creation of a lecture? Imagine a group of students clustered around the professor's cluttered desk as he or she prepares a lecture. On the desk are several sources and a crude outline. The students observe their professor deciding what purposes the lectures should fulfill and why certain substantive points and examples are chosen to emphasize and why others are discarded. To be a part of this exhilarating (and sometimes painful) process of creation is a genuine window on the mind at work. The lecture itself the next morning, by comparison, is but a show. Obviously, it is impossible to invite four hundred—or even

---

The important point is not the final chalkboard creation but the process. The participatory lecture requires less recording—and more thinking—than the oral essay.

---

forty—students into one's office or home for the time it takes to construct a good lecture. But can the process of creation be duplicated, or at least approximated, with student participation, in the classroom itself?

The participatory lecture is best described as orderly brainstorming in which students generate ideas which are then organized in some rational, coherent pattern on the chalkboard. When beginning a new topic, start with a participatory lecture by inviting students to brainstorm together by calling out "everything you know about World War I" (or Freud, Darwinism, China, waves and particles). As recorded on the blackboard (or on an overhead projection), a list will unfold of a mixture of specific facts, impressionistic feelings and prejudices, and possibly even interpretive judgments. Students bring to most courses both some familiarity and considerable misinformation, both of which can be ascertained in a participatory lecture.

The only rule of brainstorming is to acknowledge *every* offering by writing it down. As ideas are pro-

---

T he mini-lecture and discussion format counters the attention span problem by making 15–20 minute shifts in energy from the teacher to students and back again.

---

posed, you might even arrange what you hear in rough categories, but tell the students what you're doing lest you be suspected of manipulating their contributions. Better yet, once the board is filled, ask students to suggest categories and to comment on the accuracy and relative importance of the array of facts, impressions, and interpretations. Refinements can be dealt with by use of the eraser, a luxury not allowed in the formal lecture. The action of an evolving creation on the chalkboard, especially for the visually oriented learners of the television generation, reinforces learning far better than the lost words of an entirely auditory presentation.

When the class is over, an organized configuration of the ideas contributed by both students and instructor will appear on the chalkboard. Ask one student to take notes so you can run off copies for the class. The important point, however, is not the final chalkboard creation but the process. The participatory lecture differs from the oral essay by requiring more thinking and less recording. Ideally, students spend their time not transcribing or doodling but concentrating on contributing

to the evolving creation in front of them. Obviously, the participatory lecture can be done badly. When students have not brought to the class the limited knowledge provided by their prior experience or reading, or when the professor manipulates student statements to a rigidly preconceived schema, the experience can be dreary.

But when the mutual participation is free and open, students are actively engaged and teachers might even learn new insights about familiar material. Roles are blurred and all become learners and teachers. Although obviously less efficient than an oral essay, what is important is that the participatory lecture involves many students actively and *can be done with large classes.*

In a sense, all the remaining variations are versions of the participatory lecture and involve varying degrees of faculty-student interaction. It is the presence of *some* interaction, especially in large lecture courses, that students and recent critics of undergraduate education have been calling for. Martin J. Finklestein's synthesis of recent research on student evaluations concludes that "the teaching practices that a faculty member adopts in the classroom are clearly and strongly related to perceived teaching effectiveness." In defining teaching effectiveness, students consistently rate highest those faculty who show respect for students and their progress, who pay attention to classroom processes, and who use presentational styles that encourage participation.[8]

3. Problem Solving: Demonstrations, Proofs, and Stories

> What brought the two former friends, one in blue and one in grey, to oppose each other on Cemetery Ridge in Gettysburg that hot July afternoon?

This lecture begins with a question, or a paradox, or an enigma, or a compellingly unfinished human story—some tantalizing problem that hooks student interest. The answer unfolds during the class hour; if skillful the unfolding will be completed with only about ten or fewer minutes left in the period. Solving the problem, depending on what it is or in what field, may require a scientific demonstration, a mathematical proof, an economic model, the outcome of the novel's plot, or an his-

torical narrative. The question is woven throughout the lecture, inviting students to fill in imaginative spaces in the story (or model) with their own unfolding solutions to the problem.

The unfolding can consist primarily of a lecture, in which students fill in their successive answers passively, or of an interactive process in which students' tentative solutions to a problem, or completions of a story, are elicited, listed on the board, and discussed. "What do you think will happen?" "Which solution, outcome, or explanation makes the most sense to you?" If no consensus, the teacher lectures a little more, invites a new set of student responses, and asks the question again. Ideally, when the problem is finally resolved, most students will have figured it out themselves just before the teacher's solution is announced.

4. Energy Shifts: Alternating Mini-Lectures and Discussions

I firmly believe that the flow of energy around a class-room has a great deal to do with how well students learn. The following variation, which is similar to the participatory and problem-solving lectures, recognizes the conclusions of attention span studies by making clearly delineated 15–20 minute shifts in energy from the teacher to students and back again. The instructor begins with a 20-minute lecture setting the stage for some issue, which involves a 10–15 minute discussion of implications and effects, followed by another mini-lecture on what happened next. The last 5 minutes might be spent by presenting students with an assignment: a problem or application of the issues raised in the second mini-lecture. Thus, the next class would begin with the mini-discussion, followed by a mini-lecture, etc. This alternating approach can describe any natural or social

science class where instruction calls for a mixture of theory and data, model and findings, or hypothesis and experimental demonstration, with intervening considerations of how best to proceed next. The point is to shorten segments of one method of learning, change the voices(s) heard, and shift the energy.

In a lecture hall filled with 200–400 students, the mini-discussions need not involve "breaking up into groups of five or six" (as they well might in smaller classes of 100 or less). Rather, huge classes can be handled by asking two or three students sitting next to each other to discuss the problem together for a few minutes, and then inviting volunteers to stand and report conclusions and concerns. This process provides public affirmation of the appropriate issues (or not), thus giving feedback both to other students and to the teacher on how well the students were prepared for a particular problem. Even "wrong" feedback is instructive and sharpens the focus of the next appropriate mini-lecture and reading assignment. Without the mini-discussion segment, the teacher might not have known the gaps in student knowledge and gone ahead with the next lesson, which is most serious in sequential science courses. Moreover, with energy shifts students experience a variety of voices and a sense of shared responsibility for their learning.

5. Textual Exegesis: Modeling Analytical Skills

> Jennifer, would you read the top paragraph on page 40 please?

One deficiency of undergraduate education we have been hearing about (and often experiencing) is that our students are illiterate. They do not know how to read, we are told, which is a rather necessary prerequisite for developing analytical skills. The lecture setting of any size provides an opportunity to practice an old-fashioned but underused technique: *explication du texte*. We do not often enough go to a text and read and analyze passages together out loud. Students can develop these skills by seeing them modeled, followed by an opportunity to practice analyzing a text themselves.

A class of 50 or 500 students, following along in their books, or on handouts, or on an overhead projection, can watch a professor working through selected passages of a document, speech, sermon, essay, poem, proof, or fictional passage. Upon reaching a particularly ambiguous passage, the mini-discussion in groups of 3–5 students could be employed, thus shifting the energy and providing practice and feedback for students. The professor's response to how different groups of students resolve the ambiguity ("What is Locke saying here?") furthers the learning.

This process of modeling how to read analytically can be done for other than just verbal texts. Art historians, musicologists, economists, and anthropologists have traditionally used lectures to show students how to "read" an abstract painting, sonata, supply and demand curve, or artifact. Natural scientists explain their "texts" with elaborate demonstrations (and labs for practice). What I am suggesting is that in those many courses where the mastery of traditional verbal texts is fundamental to the learning goals of the course, we use the lecture period as an opportunity to teach critical interpretation and analysis to our students—that is, how to read.

A further variation on this approach, especially for social science courses, is to use the lecture period to train students in other analytical skills—quantitative analysis of graphs, charts and tables, and how to read maps, interview schedules, or census and polling data. In sum, make sure students have a copy of the document in question in front of them (or visual access through slides and overhead transparencies), and then follow three steps: modeling by the professor, practice by the students, and feedback.

6. Cutting Large Classes in Half without Losing Control: Debates

> "But my class is too large for these gimmicks!" "I couldn't possibly let them go into those little groups in the middle of class. I wouldn't trust what they're talking about and am afraid I'd lose control."

Although assigning specific tasks to small groups of two or three students can disperse energy and achieve interaction in large classes, not all instructors would be comfortable with the uncertainty of "what they're talking about." The concern for control is a genuine and important one. Although once we open up the lecture

hall to voices other than our own we risk some diminished control over content and tone, none of these variations is intended to relinquish the teacher's control of the class. Therefore, let me suggest a few ways of achieving more student participation and engagement in large classes without changing the professor's central and vital controlling role in the classroom.

One obvious strategy is to take advantage of the central aisle dividing large lecture halls in order to structure debates. Students can either support the side of an issue assigned to the half of the hall where they happen to be

sitting, or as prearranged, come to class prepared to take a seat on one particular side of a debate. Whichever approach you use, you can maintain rigorous control from the podium in guiding the process: "From the right side of the hall we will hear five statements on behalf of the Confederacy, after which we will hear five statements from the left on behalf of the Union." The process can be repeated once or twice, including the inevitable rebuttals, before concluding by asking for two or three volunteers to make summary arguments for each side.

Although neither one of two polar sides of an issue contains the whole truth, it is pedagogically energizing and valuable (if only to point out the complexity of truth) for students to be compelled to choose and then to defend one side of a dichotomous question. Other obvious debate topics include such questions as: "Burke or Paine?" "Should Nora have left or stayed?" "Pro-life or pro-choice?" "Marx or Adam Smith?" "Waves or particles?" "Declare war or not?"

> "But most important questions do not divide into halves. . . . My students would never settle for forced choices."

When some students (quite rightly) refuse to choose one side or the other, create a middle ground and space and invite their reasons for choosing it. Students might learn how difficult it is to try to remain neutral on heated issues, especially during revolutionary times. Besides, some large lecture halls have two central aisles, which makes legitimizing a third position both intellectually defensible and physically possible. Whichever approach is used in dividing classes, the professor has maintained control and a central focus and students have added a participatory dimension to their learning in a traditional lecture setting.

7. Smaller Groups in Large Classes: Simulations and Role Playing

For those teachers willing occasionally to risk a little classroom chaos, the following variation is guaranteed to add energy, participation, and interaction to large lecture hall courses. I have written previously in this journal in more detail about using small groups and role-playing in history classes,[9] so here I will just sketch the outlines of this "lecture" variation. It is adaptable (often as simulations) to political science, economics, sociology, and other disciplines.

First, a crucial mini-lecture clearly establishes the context and setting for the role playing (defined as a loose simulation of actual actors and problems). Second, the class is divided into a number of small groups (of varying sizes and including duplicate roles depending on the overall class size), each group assigned a clearly delineated role—usually of some historical or contemporary group. Third, each group is given a

193

specific, concrete task—usually to propose a position and course of action. And fourth, the proposals emanating from different groups will inevitably conflict with each other in some way—ideologically, tactically, racially, regionally, or over scarce funds, land, jobs, power, or resources.

The format of such sessions can take whatever direction a professor wishes, given clear planning and instructions, assertive leadership, and a lot of luck. One

The first is based on Martin Duberman's 1960s drama, *In White America*, in which the historian-playwright skillfully pieced together actual quotations from the black historical experience in white America into a compellingly gripping drama. None of us is a Duberman or Arthur Miller, but we all have an eye (or a heart) for particularly moving quotations, poems, or song lyrics. Focusing on a single topic (e.g., male-female stereotypes, the Depression, work, the nature of

---

S ometimes it is better for the emotional impact of the music and images to conclude the class, letting students leave the room with their hearts thumping . . . and their motivation to study aroused.

---

might hear the proposals of different groups and immediately incorporate them into a lecture on what really happened or should happen as a result of these same conflicts and collisions. Or, one might carry out the role-playing process longer by structuring the stages of a meeting or convention that followed the initial proposals. The student groups might, for example, be instructed to prepare speeches and see the deliberations through to some conclusion, or to caucus in order to develop strategies, coalitions, and tactics for achieving their goals. Neat, simple, clear closures are not easy (short of the class-ending buzzer), but this variation for large lecture classes has tremendous potential for experiential learning and of course involves enormous energy and interaction.

When the professor wishes to bring closure, however, debriefing the exercise—which is essential—is an opportunity to restore order. The debriefing also helps to identify what was learned, and to make the transition to the next topic and pedagogical approach, probably a lecture to tie up loose ends.

8. "Bells and Whistles": The Affective, Emotional Media Lecture

Every time a colleague sees me heading off to class with my cassette recorder, and slide carousel, he says, "here come the bells and whistles." It is not intended as a compliment. No list of variations for large lecture classes is complete without acknowledging the use of media. Since much has been written on the use of films and other audio-visual techniques in teaching, I want to focus on two approaches designed to evoke an emotional involvement by affective, emotional learning, an area woefully neglected in college teaching.

warfare, or Chinese culture), put together a collage of quotations, not necessarily in any particular order. Invite some theater majors or an oral interpretation class (or some of your own students) to read the quotations in class one day, either as an extended presentation followed by a short discussion, or as a brief introduction to your lecture on the topic.

The second affective media suggestion is the synchronized slide-tape presentation, consciously matching a series of visual images with the words of a song or speech. One need not prepare a spectacular show with multiple slide images emanating from several automatically timed projectors. Rather, select two or three songs or a speech that you think captures the mood or tone of an event, era, or issue, and select some slides to represent the words, changing as each new idea in the lyrics calls for a corresponding visual image.

To be sure, the presentation, especially with music, is a blatant ploy to hook student emotions in order to arouse their interest. But there is also extensive content inherent in the visual images and lyrics. After showing five minutes of 20–25 slides to accompany two haunting Harry Chapin songs on what has happened to America since the 1960s, we go back over each slide and talk about the historical context and the meaning of each line of the lyrics, which students have on a handout. The discussion could last for hours. Sometimes though, it is better for the emotional impact of the music and images to conclude the class, letting students leave the room with their hearts thumping, their minds engaged, and their motivation to study aroused. Which, after all, has been the goal of each of these lecture variations.

It must be clear that putting together a slide-tape presentation, or a small group role-playing experience, or even a participatory lecture, takes planning time and effort, probably about as much as an exquisite oral essay or even an ordinary lecture, the one we know "could have been better but will have to do." It is important to use *all* of these different variations of the lecture, broadening our options as teachers by selecting what works for us. "The test of a good teacher," someone has said, "is how well Plan B works." To have a good Plan B for each major concept implies, of course, enlarging our repertoire.

Above all, I have sought to show in this article that large lecture hall classes need not be barriers to providing the kind of interactive, participatory experiences that enhance student learning and renew faculty commitment to the highest challenges of our calling. And who knows, after using a variety of approaches which involve students actively in the classroom, one could even finish a 30-minute lecture to a large class and ask, "Any questions?"—and be pleasantly surprised by the response.

NOTES

1. See *Integrity in the College Curriculum: A Report to the Academic Community*, Association of American Colleges, 1985; *Involvement in Learning: Realizing the Potential of American Higher Education*, National Institute of Education, 1984; and William J. Bennett, *To Reclaim a Legacy: A Report on the Humanities in Higher Education*, National Endowment for the Humanities, 1984.

2. Wilbert J. McKeachie, *Teaching Tips—A Guidebook for the Beginning College Teacher*, 6th edition (Lexington, Mass.: D.C. Heath and Co., 1969), p. 36.

3. Bette LaSere and Glenn R. Erickson, "Presenting and Explaining," unpublished manuscript, University of Rhode Island Instructional Development Program, 1984, p. 1.

4. Heather Dubrow and James Wilkinson, "The Theory and Practice of Lectures," in *The Art and Craft of Teaching*, Margaret Morganroth Gullette, ed., Harvard-Danforth Center for Teaching and Learning (Cambridge, Massachusetts: Harvard University Press, 1984), p. 25.

5. Dubrow and Wilkinson, *Art and Craft of Teaching*, p. 25.

6. Bette LaSere Erickson and Glenn Erickson's "Presenting and Explaining" contains an excellent set of specific "recommendations for planning effective presentations," p. 9.

7. David Bergman, "In Defense of Lecturing," *Association of Departments of English Bulletin* 76 (Winter, 1983), pp. 49–50.

8. Martin J. Finkelstein, *The American Academic Profession— A Synthesis of Social Scientific Inquiry Since World War II* (Columbus: Ohio State University Press, 1984), pp. 109 ff.

9. Peter Frederick, "The Dreaded Discussion: Ten Ways to Start," *Improving College and University Teaching* 29 (Summer 1981), 109-14.

"STRATEGIES for ACTIVE LEARNING in HISTORY COURSES/CLASSROOMS"

ACM/GLCA History Conference   Peter Frederick
University of Chicago   March 31, 1989   Wabash College

> *"to get them to talk . . . he had to devise schemes to find what they were thinking about . . ."*
>
> --Henry Adams

Ten Practical Strategies ("schemes") for Involving Students:

1. **Using brief writing and pairs to get started** - responses to texts, mini-lectures, historical problems - "main thesis, or issue?" "what would you do?" "what's the major cause?" "one question?"

2. **Interactive Lectures: Brainstorming** ("everything you know about slavery"), **Defining terms** ("Romanticism," "Progressivism," "Cultural Values" "Feminism"), **Problem-Solving** (e.g., Versailles - 1789 or 1919)

3. **Concrete images:** micro-events - a scene or moment, anecdotes, stories, narrative and visual images, an historical person poised at the moment of a decision ("what should the Athenians/Austrians/uncertain emigrant/Lincoln/the freedmen do?")

4. **Questions and Discussions:** from concrete to abstract, what to why, description to analysis; "a question I still have about the Holocaust is . . ." "it is true about Reconstruction that . . ." "what one thing . . .?" "the three things I now know clearly are . . ."

5. Use of **Visuals, Problems, Feedback, and Small Groups - Energy shifts**

6. **Critical thinking:** interpreting texts and documents, including even textbooks (explication du texte); identifying and exploring historical issues; making priorities and decisions; generating theses; finding the point of view

7. **"History Labs"** - artifacts and material culture, photographs and cartoons; quantitative data - tables, graphs, charts, census; maps; diaries and journals, family data . . .

8. **Debates:** dichotomous questions: "Burke or Paine?" "Booker T. or W.E.B.?" "Annex the Philippines?" "Sicily?" "Hawk or Dove?" "Calvin or Sadoleto?" - and choices among options: ("which of his many names is the essential Malcolm X?" - "what best defines American ethnicity: melting pot or salad or stew or what?" - "What course for China?")

9. **Role-playing:** from elaborate simulations to simpler roles (an historical figure) and groups (social, class, ethnic, racial, nationality, etc.) (19th century American social history)

10. **Use of Media:** Songs, speeches, slides, and emotions: to set tone, to raise questions, to deepen analysis, to make concrete, to review and rethink, to motivate, to hook their world to ours, i.e., to stimulate cognitive understanding by affective experience

11. **Others?**

ACTIVE LEARNING in the HISTORY CLASSROOM
Lecture and Discussion Strategies

Peter Frederick   **OAH**   Julie Jeffrey
Wabash College   (Reno, 1988)   Goucher College
                      (Philadelphia, 1987)

An Exchange of Ideas that Work

Tell me, and I'll listen.
Show me, and I'll understand.
Involve me, and I'll learn.
_ Lakota (Sioux)

Henry Adams's problem...

And ours...

Ten Practical Active Learning Strategies:

1.   Using brief writing and pairs to get started _ responses to
     texts, completing ideas

2.   Interactive Lectures: Brainstorming, Defining terms,
     Identifying and Solving problems

3.   Concrete images: scenes, events, moments, anecdotes, stories

4.   Use of Visuals and Small Groups--energy shifts

5.   Using Questions and Discussions: from concrete to abstract,
     description to analysis

6.   Critical thinking: interpreting texts, documents, and
     material culture artifacts in class; making priorities and
     decisions; generating theses

7.   Debates: dichotomous questions

8.   Role Playing: from Elaborate to Simple

9.   Affective Media: Songs, slides, and emotions: to set tone,
     to raise questions, to deepen analysis, to make concrete, to
     review and rethink

10. ?